fondues

fondues

over 160 step-by-step recipes

A Salamander Book

Published by Salamander Books Ltd
8 Blenheim Court Brewery Road
London N7 9NY
United Kingdom

© **Salamander Books Ltd, 2003**

A member of **Chrysalis** Books plc

ISBN: 1 84065 433 3

1 2 3 4 5 6 7 8 9 10

All correspondence concerning the content of this volume should be addressed to Salamander Books Ltd.

CREDITS
Project managed by Stella Caldwell
Editor: Madeline Weston
Typeset by SX Composing DTP, Essex

Printed in China

CONTENTS

INTRODUCTION

*Left: Large stainless
steel fondue pot*

The word fondue comes from the French word *fondre*, to melt. It was in the French speaking area of Switzerland that the cheese fondue originated many centuries ago. During the harsh Alpine winters Swiss peasants had very limited food apart from cheese and bread, and they had few cooking utensils, so melting the cheese in one pot was a good way of using up the rather dry odds and ends of cheese. The cheese fondue became widely known outside Switzerland when people began to take skiing holidays and enjoyed a fondue or raclette after a hard-day on the slopes.

Many countries around the world have developed their own version of the fondue. The classic fondue Bourguignonne, where strips of steak are cooked in hot oil, is very popular in France, while in the Far East pieces of meat, fish or chicken are cooked in boiling stock along with vegetables. Afterwards, noodles are added to the stock which is then served up as a soup.

The fondue, extremely popular in the 1970s, is making a welcome return to the stylish dinner table, and today there is a great variety of different types of fondue sets available on the market. A fondue set will usually consist of a pot, a stand on which the pot rests, and a burner for cooking or keeping the food hot. In addition to this, they often come with a set of four or six long-handled forks. The burner either contains a pad which needs to be impregnated with methylated spirits, or a foil container of gel is placed in the burner. They will usually have a sliding cover over the burner which will enable you to adjust the size of the flame. A cover is also usually provided for snuffing out the flame when cooking has been completed. Small chocolate fondue pots have a candle to provide a gentle

heat. It is extremely important that the base containing the burner is very stable and it should be placed on a thick mat on the table.

The traditional cheese fondue pot resembles the original Swiss *caquelon*; it is wide and quite shallow and usually made of earthenware and sometimes light metal such as copper. These pots are not suitable for a meat fondue as they are too open and shallow for hot oil or stock. It is quite easy to overheat the metal pots, which will cause the cheese to catch and burn.

A traditional meat fondue pot is taller and narrower, but most fondue pots sold nowadays tend to be this shape and they are suitable for either meat or cheese fondues. Cast iron pots are typically the most expensive on the market, but they are the best quality as it is much easier to keep a steady temperature with cast iron. Another advantage is that the weight of the cast iron sets makes them more stable.

Chocolate fondue sets are smaller in size but it is not necessary to have a special pot as an attractive bowl over a nightlight works just as well. A chocolate fondue set can be very useful for keeping sauces warm at the table. Similar to a chocolate fondue set is a special pot for making Bagna Cauda, and again, this is heated with the aid of a nightlight. These pots are most frequently made of terracotta.

A Mongolian hotpot or steamboat is a traditional pot in which Oriental fondues are made. They are manufactured of brass or aluminium and consist of a rounded pot which has a funnel running down the centre of it. This is set over a burner into which hot charcoal is placed. Boiling stock is used and the burner ensures it is kept bubbling throughout the meal.

Long handled forks are essential pieces of equipment for spearing whatever food is being dipped into the fondue. They most often have coloured handles or a coloured mark on the end so that each diner can readily identify their own fork. The food is transferred to a dinner plate,

Above: Small chocolate fondue pot

and dipped into one of the sauces with an eating fork before consumption. This is not just for hygiene reasons, but also to avoid people burning themselves - of particular importance when dipping food into hot oil. As an alternative to forks, bamboo skewers can also be used. Little Chinese wire baskets are used with Mongolian hotpots, but they also come in useful for dipping food such as meatballs, fishcakes or anything else which might be too fragile to stay on a fork.

Six is the maximum number of people who can safely and comfortably share one fondue pot, so for parties of eight or more it would be necessary to have two pots on the go simultaneously. For more speed, make the cheese fondue on top of the stove before transferring it to the burner. Also heat oil or stock on top of the stove and for obvious reasons take great care when transferring the fondue pot to the burner.

CHEESE FONDUES

Choose a strongly flavoured cheese and always allow it to melt slowly. You need to have alcohol in a cheese fondue. Not only does it improve the flavour, but it lowers the boiling point and stops the protein in the cheese from curdling. Do not worry if the mixture looks lumpy and separates; keep stirring and it will gradually become smooth, but do not be tempted to turn the heat up as this will probably overcook and spoil the fondue. If the mixture becomes too thick, add a little warmed wine or cider. Encourage diners to stir the fondue right down to the bottom when they dip their bread in; this helps to keep it smooth and creamy. When the fondue is nearly finished there

Right:
Cast iron
fondue pot
with spirit burner

will usually be a crisp crust on the bottom off the pot. Scrape it out and divide it between the guests - it tastes wonderful and is regarded as a treat. Make use of day-old bread for dipping as it will not be too crumbly, and always cut the bread so that each portion has some crust on to make spearing with a fork easier. If anybody does drop their bread in the fondue, tradition dictates that they have to perform a forfeit. Ladies have to kiss the man next to them and a man is obliged to buy the next round of drinks!

MEAT, FISH AND SEAFOOD FONDUES

It is important to have all the ingredients and accompaniments prepared in advance; this makes your task much easier. The meat should be cut and arranged attractively on plates, sauces need to be prepared and placed in small pots, and salads should be ready for dressing just before cooking commences. If using oil, vegetable oil is recommended, but a little flavoured oil can be added if you like. For safety reasons, the fondue pot should not be filled more than half full as the hot oil can easily bubble up when the meat is dipped in. Heat the oil to 180-190C (350-375F), but if you do not have a thermometer to hand, there is an quick and easy test which you can perform using a piece of day-old bread. Dip a small cube into the oil; it will turn golden in about 30 seconds if the oil is at the correct temperature. Be careful not to add too much food to the oil at once. This will have the effect of lowering the temperature of the oil and the food will consequently not cook properly. Dry meat and fish on kitchen paper before cooking in hot oil, otherwise the oil will spit.

DESSERT FONDUES

Most dessert fondues are made of chocolate, but creamy fruit purées are

popular too. Melted chocolate is luxurious, silky-smooth and offers a great feel-good factor. It always pays to choose the best quality - for cooking purposes, a rich, dark chocolate is recommended. Always check the label for cocoa-solid content, and try not to go below 50 per cent. Take great care when melting the chocolate, especially if it is white chocolate, as it will solidify into clumps if overheated. Melting the chocolate with cream solves this problem and makes for a delicious mixture!

If you are dipping cake into the fondue, freshly baked cake can be a little too crumbly. Day-old cake works best, so if you are planning to make one of the dessert fondues with small cakes or cake slices, it is a good idea to prepare the cake the day before. If you are dipping fruit, choose firm pieces and, if possible, chill them first as the chocolate will coat them more effectively when they are cold.

CHEESE

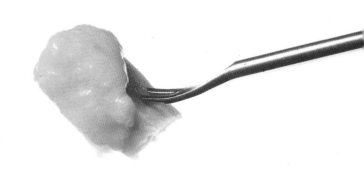

FONDUE SAVOYARDE

1 clove garlic, halved
150ml (5fl oz/⅔ cup) dry white wine
1 teaspoon lemon juice
225g (8oz/2 cups) grated Gruyère cheese
225g (8oz/2 cups) grated Emmental cheese
1 tablespoon cornflour
2 tablespoons kirsch
pinch freshly grated nutmeg
pinch cayenne pepper
TO SERVE:
cubes of baguette
green salad
slices of air dried ham

Rub cut side of garlic round inside fondue pot.

Pour wine and lemon juice into the pot and place over a low heat. Heat gently until bubbling. Gradually stir in grated cheeses and heat gently, stirring, until completely melted. In a small bowl, blend together the cornflour and kirsch and stir into cheese mixture.

Continue to cook, stirring, for 2-3 minutes until mixture is thick and creamy. Add nutmeg and cayenne pepper. Transfer pot to the lighted spirit burner. To serve, spear cubes of bread on to the fondue forks and dip into cheese mixture. Serve with the salad and air dried ham.

Serves 4-6.

DEVILLED CHEESE FONDUE

1 clove garlic, cut in half
175ml (6fl oz/¾ cup) milk
375g (13oz/3 cups) grated Applewood smoked Cheddar cheese
6 teaspoons plain flour
1 teaspoon prepared mustard
2 teaspoons Worcestershire sauce
2 teaspoons horseradish relish
cubes of ham and toasted granary bread, to serve

Rub the inside of the fondue pot with the cut clove of garlic, then add milk and heat until bubbling.

Toss the cheese in the flour, then add to the pot and stir all the time over a low heat until it is melted and mixture is thick and smooth.

Stir in the mustard, Worcestershire sauce and horseradish relish. Serve with cubes of ham and cubes of toasted granary bread.

Serves 4-6.

CLASSIC SWISS FONDUE

1 clove garlic, halved
225ml (8fl oz/1 cup) dry white wine
1 teaspoon lemon juice
225g (8oz/2 cups) grated Gruyère cheese
225g (8oz/2 cups) grated Emmental cheese
2 teaspoons cornflour
2 tablespoons kirsch
pinch white pepper
pinch freshly grated nutmeg
cubes of French bread, to serve

Rub the inside of the fondue pot with cut clove of garlic.

Pour in wine and lemon juice and heat gently until bubbling. Reduce the heat to low and gradually stir in grated cheese with a wooden spoon, then continue to heat until cheeses melt, stirring frequently.

In a small bowl, blend cornflour smoothly with kirsch, then stir in cheese mixture and continue to cook for 2-3 minutes until mixture of thick and smooth, stirring frequently. Do not allow fondue to boil. Season with pepper and nutmeg. Serve with cubes of French bread.

Serves 4-6.

GOUDA CHEESE FONDUE

½ small onion
2 teaspoons cumin seeds
150ml (5fl oz/⅔ cup) dry white wine
1 teaspoon lemon juice
400g (14oz/3½ cups) grated Gouda cheese
2 teaspoons cornflour
2 tablespoons gin
freshly ground black pepper
pinch nutmeg
light rye bread cubes, to serve

Rub inside of the fondue pot with cut side of onion. Place cumin seeds in pot and heat gently for 1 minute.
Add wine and lemon juice. Heat until nearly

boiling and then add grated cheese. Heat gently, stirring, until cheese melts. In a small bowl blend together cornflour and gin. Stir into cheese mixture.

As soon as fondue thickens and comes just to a simmer, take off the heat. Season with pepper and nutmeg. Place the fondue pot over the lighted spirit burner and serve with the rye bread.

Serves 4.

FONDUE INDIENNE

1 clove garlic, halved
350g (12oz/3 cups) grated Cheddar cheese
2 tablespoons plain flour
1 small onion, grated
300ml (10fl oz/1½ cups) dry white wine
2 teaspoons curry paste
2 tablespoons mango chutney
salt and freshly ground black pepper
cayenne pepper, to garnish
naan bread, to serve

Rub the inside of the fondue pot with the cut clove of garlic. Crush the garlic.

Place cheese and flour in a plastic bag and toss to combine. Place crushed garlic, onion, wine and curry paste in the fondue pot and bring almost to a simmer. Gradually stir in cheese, allowing it to melt between each addition.

Stir in mango chutney and salt and pepper to taste. Place on the lighted spirit burner. Sprinkle a little cayenne pepper over. Serve with pieces of naan bread.

Serves 4.

Note: If the mango chutney has large pieces of fruit in it, chop it finely.

SMOKY GERMAN FONDUE

½ small onion
225ml (8fl oz/1 cup) light ale
350g (12oz/3 cups) grated German smoked cheese
115g (4oz/1 cup) grated Emmental cheese
3 teaspoons cornflour
3 tablespoons milk
1 teaspoon German mustard
rye bread and cooked frankfurters, to serve

Rub the inside of the fondue pot with cut side of onion.

Pour in ale and heat gently until bubbling. Reduce the heat to low and gradually stir in the grated cheeses, then continue to heat until cheeses melt, stirring frequently.

In a small bowl, blend cornflour smoothly with milk, stir into cheese with mustard and continue to cook for 2-3 minutes until mixture is thick and creamy, stirring frequently. Serve with cubes of rye bread and pieces of cooked frankfurters.

Serves 4-6.

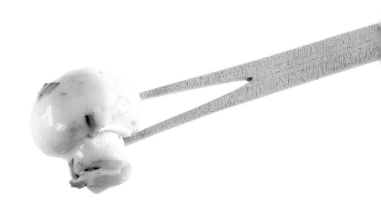

SOMERSET FONDUE

½ small onion
225ml (8fl oz/1 cup) dry cider
1 teaspoon lemon juice
350g (12oz/3 cups) grated Cheddar cheese
½ teaspoon dry mustard
3 teaspoons cornflour
3 tablespoons apple juice
pinch white pepper
wedges of apple and cubes of crusty bread, to serve

Rub the inside of the fondue pot with cut side of onion.

Pour in cider and lemon juice and heat gently until bubbling. Reduce the heat to low and gradually stir in grated cheese, then continue to heat until cheese melts, stirring frequently.

In a small bowl, blend mustard and cornflour smoothly with apple juice. Stir into cheese mixture and continue to cook for 2-3 minutes until mixture is thick and creamy, stirring frequently. Season with pepper. Serve with wedges of apple and cubes of crusty bread.

Serves 4-6.

FRENCH BRIE FONDUE

375g (13oz) ripe French Brie
50g (2oz/¼ cup) butter
1 onion, finely chopped
1 clove garlic, crushed
25g (1oz/¼ cup) plain flour
300ml (10fl oz/1¼ cups) chicken or vegetable stock
150ml (5fl oz/⅔ cup) double cream
1 tablespoon chopped fresh tarragon
salt and freshly ground black pepper
TO SERVE:
grapes
cubes of French bread
raw button mushrooms

Cut away rind from Brie and slice cheese thinly. Set aside.

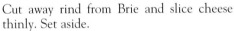

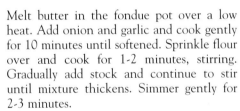

Melt butter in the fondue pot over a low heat. Add onion and garlic and cook gently for 10 minutes until softened. Sprinkle flour over and cook for 1-2 minutes, stirring. Gradually add stock and continue to stir until mixture thickens. Simmer gently for 2-3 minutes.

Stir sliced Brie and cream into the fondue. Cook, stirring, until cheese has melted and mixture is smooth. Stir in tarragon and season with salt and pepper. Transfer the fondue pot to the lighted spirit burner. To serve, spear grapes, bread and mushrooms on to skewers or fondue forks and dip into the fondue.

Serves 4-6.

SMOKY CHEESE & HAM FONDUE

115g (4oz/1 cup) grated Gruyère cheese
225g (8oz/2 cups) grated smoked Cheddar cheese
1 tablespoon cornflour
15g (½oz/1 tablespoon) butter
1 small onion, finely chopped
1 clove garlic, crushed
150ml (5fl oz/⅔ cup) dry white wine
½ teaspoon smoked paprika
115g (4oz) smoked ham, chopped
TO SERVE:
wedges of apple
cubes of crusty bread

In a bowl, toss together the grated cheese and the cornflour.

In a saucepan, melt butter over a low heat. Add onion and garlic and cook gently for 10 minutes until softened. Place wine in the fondue pot and heat gently until bubbling. Gradually stir in grated cheeses and heat gently, stirring, until completely melted.

Stir in onion and garlic, then the paprika and ham and cook for a few more minutes until thick and smooth. Transfer the fondue pot to the lighted spirit burner. To serve, spear apple and bread on to skewers or fondue forks and dip into the fondue.

Serves 4.

CHEESE & ONION FONDUE

25g (1oz/6 teaspoons) butter
1 large onion, very finely chopped
2 teaspoons plain flour
150ml (5fl oz/⅔ cup) thick sour cream
225g (8oz/2 cups) grated Gruyère cheese
225g (8oz/2 cups) grated Cheddar cheese
2 tablespoons chopped fresh chives
freshly ground black pepper
small cooked potatoes and small cooked sausages, to serve

Melt butter in a saucepan, add onion and cook for 4-5 minutes until soft but not brown.

Stir in flour, then add thick sour cream and cook for 2 minutes. Continue to cook whilst adding cheeses and heat until mixture is smooth, stirring frequently.

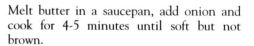

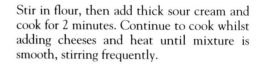

Add chives and season with pepper. Pour into the fondue pot and serve with small cooked potatoes and small cooked sausages.

Serves 4-6.

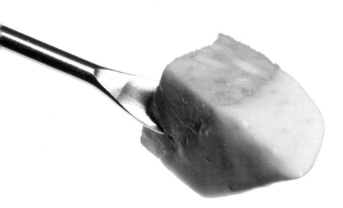

BLUE CHEESE FONDUE

225ml (8fl oz/1 cup) milk
225g (8oz/1 cup) cream cheese
225g (8oz/2 cups) grated Danish Blue cheese
½ teaspoon garlic salt
3 teaspoons cornflour
2 tablespoons single cream
cubes of ham or garlic sausage and cubes of crusty
   bread, to serve

Put milk and cream cheese into the fondue pot and, with an electric mixer, beat until creamy and smooth.

Place fondue pot over a gentle heat and gradually stir in the blue cheese, then continue to heat until smooth, stirring.

Blend garlic salt and cornflour smoothly with cream; stir into cheese and cook for a further 2-3 minutes until thick and creamy, stirring frequently. Serve with cubes of ham or garlic sausage and cubes of crusty bread.

Serves 4-6.

CIDER FONDUE

½ small onion
300ml (10fl oz/1¼ cups) dry cider
1 teaspoon lemon juice
450g (1lb/4 cups) grated farmhouse Cheddar cheese
1 tablespoon cornflour
2 tablespoons dry sherry
pinch mustard powder
1 teaspoon Worcestershire sauce
1 teaspoon chopped fresh sage
salt and freshly ground black pepper
TO SERVE:
cubes of crusty farmhouse bread
wedges of apple
celery sticks
pickle

Rub inside of the fondue pot with the cut side of onion. Place cider and lemon juice in fondue pot and heat gently until bubbling. Gradually stir in grated cheese and heat gently, stirring, until completely melted. In a small bowl, blend together cornflour and sherry. Add mustard and Worcestershire sauce. Stir into cheese mixture.

Continue to cook, stirring until thick and smooth. Stir in sage and season with salt and pepper. Transfer the fondue pot to the lighted spirit burner. To serve, spear bread on to fondue forks to dip into fondue and serve accompanied by apple, celery and pickle.

Serves 6.

ITALIAN PESTO FONDUE

1 clove garlic
200ml (7fl oz/scant 1 cup) Soave wine
225g (8oz/2 cups) grated Gruyère cheese
175g (6oz/1½ cups) dolcelatte cheese, cubed
50g (2oz/½ cup) grated Parmesan cheese
1 tablespoon cornflour
2 tablespoons milk
1 tablespoon pesto sauce
salt and freshly ground black pepper
TO SERVE:
foccacia and ciabatta bread cut into cubes
slices of salami
olives

Cut clove of garlic in half and rub cut side round the inside of the fondue pot. (See above.) Place wine in the fondue pot and heat gently until bubbling. Gradually stir in prepared cheeses and heat gently, stirring, until completely melted. In a small bowl, blend together the cornflour and milk. Stir into the cheese mixture. Continue to cook, stirring, until thick and smooth.

Stir in pesto and season with salt and pepper. Transfer the fondue pot to the lighted spirit burner. To serve, spear bread and salami on to fondue forks to dip into the fondue and serve accompanied by the olives.

Serves 6.

VARIATION: Instead of bread and salami, serve cooked tortelloni to dip into the fondue.

DUTCH FONDUE

½ small onion
225ml (8fl oz/1 cup) milk
450g (1lb/4 cups) grated Gouda cheese
2 teaspoons caraway seeds
3 teaspoons cornflour
3 tablespoons gin
freshly ground black pepper
light rye bread and button mushrooms, to serve

Rub the inside of the fondue pot with cut side of onion.

Add milk and heat until bubbling, then gradually stir in cheese. Continue to heat until cheese melts, stirring frequently.

Stir in caraway seeds. In a small bowl, blend cornflour smoothly with gin, then stir into cheese mixture and cook for 2-3 minutes until smooth and creamy, stirring frequently. Season with pepper. Serve with cubes of rye bread and mushrooms.

Serves 4-6.

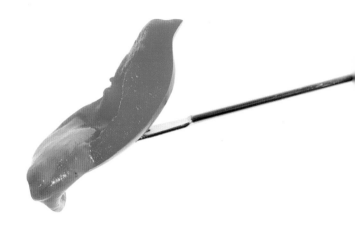

FONDUE ITALIENNE

1 clove garlic
300ml (10fl oz/1¼ cups) milk
225g (8oz/2 cups) grated Mozzarella cheese
225g (8oz/2 cups) dolcelatte cheese, chopped
50g (2oz/½ cup) finely grated Parmesan cheese
2 teaspoons cornflour
3 tablespoons dry white wine
salami, breadsticks and olives, to serve

Rub the inside of the fondue pot with cut clove of garlic. Add milk and heat until bubbling.

Stir in all the cheeses and continue to heat until melted, stirring frequently.

Blend cornflour smoothly with wine, stir into cheese mixture and cook for 2-3 minutes until thick and creamy, stirring frequently. Serve with slices of rolled up salami or cubes of salami, breadsticks and olives.

Serves 4-6.

SPANISH FONDUE

1 clove garlic
250ml (9fl oz/generous 1 cup) dry Spanish white wine
225g (8oz/2 cups) grated Gruyère cheese
225g (8oz/2 cups) grated Manchego cheese
1 tablespoon cornflour
2 tablespoons dry sherry
2 teaspoons smoked Spanish paprika
salt and freshly ground black pepper
TO SERVE:
chunks of chorizo sausage
pieces of red pepper
cubes of crusty country bread
olives
cubes of membrillo (quince paste)

Cut clove of garlic in half and rub the cut side round inside of the fondue pot. Place wine in the fondue pot and heat gently until bubbling. (See above.) Gradually stir in the prepared cheeses and heat gently, stirring, until completely melted. In a small bowl, blend together cornflour and sherry. Stir into the cheese mixture. Continue to cook, stirring until thick and smooth.

Stir in paprika and season with salt and pepper. Transfer the fondue pot to the lighted spirit burner. To serve, spear chorizo sausage, pepper and bread on to fondue forks to dip into the fondue and serve accompanied by olives and membrillo.

Serves 4-6.

HIGHLAND FONDUE

WELSH RAREBIT FONDUE

1 small onion, finely chopped
15g (½oz/3 teaspoons) butter
225ml (8fl oz/1 cup) milk
450g (1lb/4 cups) grated Scottish or mature Cheddar
  cheese
3 teaspoons cornflour
4 tablespoons whisky
cubes of rye and onion bread, to serve

Put onion and butter into a saucepan and cook over a gentle heat until soft. Add milk and heat until bubbling.

15g (½oz/1 tablespoon) butter
1 small onion, finely chopped
300ml (10fl oz/1½ cups) light ale
225g (8oz/2 cups) grated Caerphilly cheese
115g (4oz/1 cup) grated Welsh Cheddar cheese
1 tablespoon cornflour
2 tablespoons milk
1 teaspoon Dijon mustard
1 teaspoon Worcestershire sauce
pinch cayenne pepper
salt and freshly ground black pepper
thick slices of toast, cut into cubes, to serve

Place butter in the fondue pot and melt over a low heat.

Gradually stir in cheese and continue to cook until melted, stirring frequently.

Add onion and cook gently for 10 minutes until softened. Add light ale and heat gently until bubbling. Gradually stir in grated cheeses and heat gently, stirring, until completely melted. In a small bowl, mix together the cornflour and milk. Stir into cheese mixture.

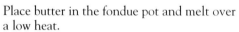

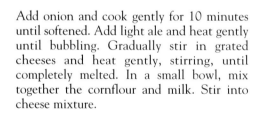

In a small bowl, blend cornflour smoothly with whisky, then stir into cheese mixture and cook 2-3 minutes until thickened, stirring frequently. Pour into the fondue pot and serve with cubes of rye and onion bread.

Serves 4-6.

Continue to cook, stirring, until thick and smooth. Stir in mustard, Worcestershire sauce and cayenne pepper. Season with salt and pepper. Transfer the fondue pot to the lighted spirit burner. To serve, spear cubes of toasted bread on fondue forks and dip into fondue.

Serves 4-6.

ISRAELI FONDUE

2 avocados, halved and stoned
3 teaspoons lemon juice
1 clove garlic, halved
175ml (6fl oz/¾ cup) dry white wine
350g (12oz/3 cups) grated Edam cheese
2 teaspoons cornflour
5 tablespoons smetana or thick sour cream
cubes of sesame-coated French bread and red and
    green pepper, to serve

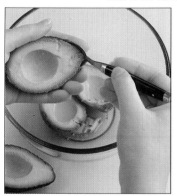

Scoop out flesh from avocados into a bowl
and mash until smooth with lemon juice.

Rub the inside of fondue pot with cut side of
garlic, then pour in wine and heat until
bubbling. Over a gentle heat, stir in cheese
and cook until melted, stirring frequently.

In a small bowl, blend cornflour smoothly
with smetana or sour cream, then add to
cheese mixture with mashed avocados.
Continue to cook for 4-5 minutes until thick
and smooth, stirring frequently. Serve with
cubes of bread and red and green pepper.

Serves 4-6.

WELSH FONDUE

225g (1oz/6 teaspoons) butter
225g (8oz) leeks, finely chopped
6 teaspoons plain flour
225ml (8fl oz/1 cup) lager
300g (10oz/2½ cups) grated Caerphilly cheese
freshly ground black pepper
cubes of crusty bread, to serve

Put butter into a saucepan and melt over a
low heat. Add leeks, cover pan and cook
gently for 10 minutes until tender.

Stir in flour and cook for 1 minute, then add
lager and heat until thickened, stirring all
the time.

Gradually add cheese and continue to cook
until melted, stirring frequently. Season with
pepper. Pour into a fondue pot and serve
with cubes of crusty bread.

Serves 4-6.

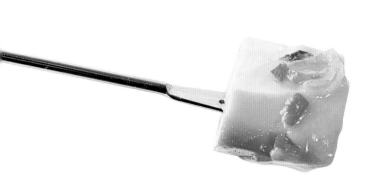

MEXICAN CHILLI FONDUE

450g (1lb/4 cups) grated Monterey Jack cheese
2 tablespoons cornflour
1 clove garlic
250ml (9fl oz/generous 1 cup) Mexican lager
1 tablespoon lime juice
1-2 fresh red chillies, seeded and finely chopped
salt and freshly ground black pepper
1 tablespoon chopped fresh coriander
FRIED SHALLOTS:
8 shallots, thinly sliced
4 tablespoons vegetable oil
TO SERVE:
pickled jalapeño chillies
tomato wedges
cubes of avocado
warm flour tortillas

Make the fried shallots. Heat oil in a frying pan, add shallots and cook, stirring, for 5 minutes or until browned. (See above.) Drain on kitchen paper and set aside. In a bowl, toss together the grated cheese and the cornflour. Cut clove of garlic in half and rub cut side round inside of the fondue pot. Add lager, lime juice and chillies and heat gently until bubbling.

Gradually stir in grated cheese and cook gently, stirring, until completely melted. Season with salt and pepper. Stir in chopped coriander and fried shallots. Transfer the fondue pot to the lighted spirit burner. Cut tortillas into strips, roll up and spear on to fondue forks to dip into the fondue, with the jalapeño chillies, tomato and avocado.

Serves 4-6.

DANISH FONDUE

175g (6oz) lean middle bacon, rind removed and finely chopped
1 small onion, finely chopped
15g (½oz/3 teaspoons) butter
3 teaspoons plain flour
225ml (8fl oz/1 cup) lager
225g (8oz/2 cups) grated Havarti cheese
225g (8oz/2 cups) grated Samso cheese
small sweet and sour gherkins and chunks of light rye bread, to serve

Put bacon, onion and butter into a saucepan and cook until bacon is golden and onion is soft.

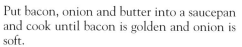

Stir in flour, then gradually add lager and cook until thickened, stirring frequently.

Add cheeses, stirring all the time, and continue cooking until cheeses have melted and mixture is smooth. Pour into a fondue pot and serve with gherkins and chunks of light rye bread.

Serves 4-6.

CREAMY HERB & GARLIC FONDUE

1 clove garlic
150ml (5fl oz/⅔ cup) dry white wine
1 tablespoon cornflour
300ml (10fl oz/1¼ cups) crème fraîche
300g (10oz/1¼ cups) full fat soft cheese with garlic
  and herbs
pinch freshly grated nutmeg
salt and freshly ground black pepper
1 tablespoon chopped fresh chives
TO SERVE:
cubes of French bread
cherry tomatoes and button mushrooms

Cut clove of garlic in half and rub the cut side round the inside of the fondue pot.

Pour 115ml (4fl oz/½ cup) of the wine into the fondue pot and heat gently until bubbling. In a small bowl, blend cornflour with the remaining wine. Add to the fondue pot and cook, stirring until thickened. Reduce the heat and add crème fraîche and soft cheese. Stir until cheese has melted.

Add nutmeg and season with salt and pepper. Sprinkle with chopped chives and transfer the fondue pot to the lighted spirit burner. To serve, spear bread, tomatoes and mushrooms on to fondue forks and dip into the fondue.

Serves 4-6.

FONDUE NORMANDE

1 clove garlic, halved
115ml (4fl oz/½ cup) dry white wine
150ml (5fl oz/⅔ cup) single cream
350g (12oz) Camembert cheese, rind removed
3 teaspoons cornflour
4 tablespoons Calvados brandy
cubes of French bread and chunks of apple, to serve

Rub the inside of fondue pot with cut side of garlic. Pour in wine and cream and heat until bubbling.

Cut cheese into small pieces, then add to the pot and stir over a gentle heat until melted.

In a small bowl, blend cornflour smoothly with Calvados, then add to cheese mixture and continue to cook for 2-3 minutes until thick and creamy, stirring frequently. Serve with cubes of French bread and chunks of apple.

Serves 4-6.

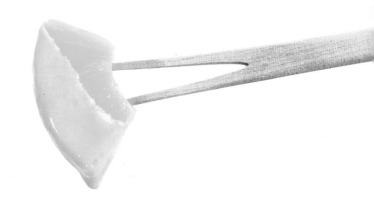

CELEBRATION FONDUE

1 clove garlic, halved
225ml (8fl oz/1 cup) sparkling white wine
115g (4oz/1 cup) grated Emmental cheese
350g (12oz/3 cups) grated Saint Paulin cheese
2 egg yolks
4 tablespoons single cream
2 teaspoons cornflour
2 tablespoons brandy
Bresaola and cubes of French bread, to serve

Rub the inside of fondue pot with cut clove of garlic. Add wine and heat until bubbling.

Gradually add cheeses and heat until melting, then beat in egg yolks and cream.

In a small bowl, blend cornflour smoothly with brandy, then add to cheese mixture and continue to cook, stirring all the time, until the fondue is thick and creamy. Serve with rolls of Bresaola and cubes of bread.

Serves 4-6.

CHILDREN'S PARTY FONDUE

25g (1oz/2 tablespoons) butter
25g (1oz/¼ cup) plain flour
450ml (16fl oz/2 cups) milk
115g (4oz/½ cup) cream cheese
175g (6oz/1½ cups) grated Edam cheese
100ml (3½fl oz/scant ½ cup) double cream
½ teaspoon dry mustard
salt and freshly ground black pepper
TO SERVE:
carrot and celery sticks
cherry tomatoes
spring onions
wedges of apple
pineapple cubes
cooked baby potatoes

Arrange vegetables and fruit on individual serving plates. Place butter in the fondue pot and heat until melted. (See above.) Stir in flour and cook, stirring for 1 minute. Gradually stir in milk, then bring to the boil and cook, stirring, until thickened and smooth. Stir in cream cheese, Edam cheese and cream. Heat gently, stirring, until cheese has melted and mixture is smooth.

Stir in mustard and season with salt and pepper. Transfer the fondue pot to the lighted spirit burner. To serve, spear vegetables and fruit on to fondue forks and dip into the fondue.

Serves 5-6.

CRICKETER'S FONDUE

15g (½oz/3 teaspoons) butter
1 small onion, finely chopped
225ml (8fl oz/1 cup) light ale
450g (1lb/4 cups) grated Leicestershire cheese
4 teaspoons cornflour
5 tablespoons single cream
cauliflower florets, radishes and mushrooms, to serve

Heat butter in a saucepan, add onion and cook gently until soft. Pour in ale and heat until bubbling.

Over a low heat, stir in the cheese and continue to heat until cheese has melted, stirring frequently.

In a small bowl, blend cornflour smoothly with cream, add to cheese mixture and cook for 2-3 minutes until smooth and thickened, stirring frequently. Pour into a fondue pot. Serve with cauliflower florets, radishes and mushrooms.

Serves 4-6.

ROSÉ FONDUE

1 clove garlic, halved
225ml (8fl oz/1 cup) rosé wine
115g (4oz/1 cup) grated Gruyère cheese
225g (8oz/2 cups) grated red-veined Cheddar cheese
3 teaspoons cornflour
2 tablespoons kirsch
cubes of sesame-coated French bread, to serve

Rub the inside of the fondue pot with cut side of garlic. Add wine and heat until bubbling.

Gradually stir in cheeses and continue to heat gently until melted, stirring frequently.

In a small bowl, blend cornflour smoothly with kirsch and stir into cheese mixture. Cook for 2-3 minutes until smooth and thickened, stirring frequently. Serve with cubes of French bread.

Serves 4-6.

PLOUGHMAN'S FONDUE

1 clove garlic, halved
300ml (10fl oz/1¼cups) beer
225g (8oz/2 cups) grated Red Leicester cheese or
   orange-coloured Cheddar
225g (8oz/2 cups) grated Cheddar cheese
3 teaspoons plain flour
1 teaspoon dry mustard
freshly ground black pepper
cubes of granary of white bread and pickles, to serve

Rub the inside of the fondue pot with cut clove of garlic. Add beer and heat until bubbling.

Toss grated cheeses in the flour and mustard until well combined.

Over a low heat, add cheeses to the beer and continue to heat, stirring all the time until mixture is smooth. Season with pepper. Serve with cubes of granary or white bread and pickles.

Serves 4-6.

CRUNCHY CAMEMBERT

12 x 25g (1oz) portions Camembert
2 eggs, beaten
115g (4oz/1 cup) dried breadcrumbs
oil, for cooking
BLUEBERRY SAUCE:
2 teaspoons cornflour
225g (8oz) blueberries, thawed if frozen
50g (2oz/¼ cup) sugar
2 teaspoons lemon juice
sprig of mint, to garnish

Freeze the Camembert portions for 1 hour. Dip each cheese portion in egg, then in breadcrumbs. Dip portions again in egg and crumbs. Put on a plate; chill until needed.

To make blueberry sauce, in a saucepan blend cornflour smoothly with 85ml (3fl oz/ ⅓ cup) water. Add remaining ingredients and simmer until the liquid thickens, stirring all the time. Serve warm.

Heat oil in the fondue pot on top of the stove then transfer to the lighted spirit burner. The Camembert portions are cooked in hot oil at the table, using Chinese wire strainers if possible to lift them out of the pot (fondue forks will pierce the crust and cause cheese to ooze out). Serve with the sauce. Garnish with a sprig of mint.

Serves 6.

ALPINE TARTIFLETTE

RACLETTE

butter, for greasing
350g (12oz) potatoes, scrubbed
25g (1oz/2 tablespoons) butter
1 small onion, chopped
115g (4oz) smoked bacon, cut into small pieces
1 Reblochon cheese
salt and freshly ground black pepper
5 tablespoons single cream
green salad, to serve

1kg (2lb) small new potatoes
salt and freshly ground black pepper
450g (1lb) Raclette cheese
TO SERVE:
air dried ham
salami
pickled gherkins

Preheat the oven to 220C (425F/Gas 7). Butter a gratin dish. Place scrubbed potatoes in a pan of cold water and bring to the boil.

Scrub potatoes and place in a pan of cold salted water. Bring to the boil and cook for 10-15 minutes until tender. Drain and place in a warm serving bowl. Season with salt and pepper.

Cook for 15-20 minutes until tender. Drain, and when cool enough to handle, peel and cut into thick slices. Meanwhile, heat butter in a frying pan. Add onion and cook for a few minutes until soft. Add bacon and cook until lightly browned. Remove onion and bacon with a slotted spoon, drain on paper towels and set aside. Add potato slices to the pan and cook for 2-3 minutes on each side, until golden.

To cook the cheese, slice cheese thinly and place a layer of slices on a shallow metal tray and place under a hot grill until it starts to melt. Scrape the top melted layer of cheese off with a palette knife.

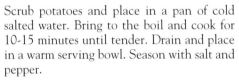

Cut the Reblochon in half and then into cubes, leaving the crust on. Make layers of potato, bacon, onion and cheese, seasoning each layer with salt and pepper. Pour cream over the top and cook in the oven for 10-12 minutes or until the top has browned. Serve with green salad.

Serves 2.

Place melted cheese on top of potatoes. Continue to cook the remaining cheese in the same way. Serve with the ham, salami and gherkins.

Serves 4.

CHEESE FONDUE TARTS

425g (15oz) puff pastry
200g (7oz/1¾ cups) grated Beaufort cheese
200g (7oz/1¾ cups) grated Jarlsberg cheese
1 clove garlic, crushed
150ml (5fl oz/⅔ cup) single cream
1 tablespoon lemon juice
2 teaspoons cornflour
3 tablespoons vodka
salt and freshly ground black pepper
2 tablespoons chopped fresh chives

Preheat the oven to 220C (425F/Gas 7). On a floured surface, roll the pastry out to 3mm (⅛in) thick and cut out twelve 10cm (4in) circles.

Place circles in a 12 hole muffin tin. Prick bases and chill for 10 minutes. Press foil into pastry cases and fill with baking beans. Bake for 15-20 minutes and remove foil and beans then bake for 5 more minutes until golden.

Meanwhile, put grated cheeses, garlic, cream and lemon juice in a pan. Cook over a gentle heat, stirring, until smooth. In a small bowl combine cornflour and vodka, add to cheese mixture and cook for 2 minutes. Season with salt and pepper and stir in chives. Divide cheese fondue between the pastry cases and serve at once.

Makes 12.

BAKED CAMEMBERT

1 small whole Camembert cheese in its box
2 cloves garlic
2 tablespoons dry white wine (optional)
chunks of crusty bread, to serve
BACON-WRAPPED POTATOES:
16 small new potatoes weighing about 450g (1lb)
salt
8 rashers streaky bacon, rinds removed
1 teaspoon Dijon mustard

Preheat the oven to 200C (400F/Gas 6). Prepare potatoes. Scrub them and place in a pan of salted water. Bring to the boil and boil for 10-15 minutes until tender. Drain.

Meanwhile, remove cheese from its box and take off the paper wrapping. Replace cheese in the box. Peel garlic cloves and cut into slivers. Push garlic slivers into the surface of cheese. Drizzle wine over, if using, so that it soaks into the holes. Replace wooden lid and bake the cheese in the oven for 25-30 minutes until bubbling.

Cut each bacon rasher in half across. Stretch out slightly with the back of a knife and smear with a little mustard. Wrap a piece of bacon round each potato and secure with a cocktail stick. Grill potatoes, turning once, until bacon is brown and crisp. Serve cheese in its box with bacon wrapped potatoes and crusty bread.

Serves 2-3.

FISH

CARIBBEAN FISH FONDUE

2 teaspoons hot pepper sauce
2 teaspoons soft brown sugar
1 teaspoon crushed allspice
1 clove garlic, crushed
½ teaspoon ground coriander
juice 1 lime
700g (1½lb) cod loin
550ml (20fl oz/2½ cups) coconut milk
1 Scotch bonnet chilli
salt
MANGO SALSA:
1 mango, peeled and finely diced
½ small red onion, finely diced
1 fresh red chilli, seeded and finely chopped
3 tablespoons chopped fresh coriander
grated rind and juice 1 lime

In a bowl, mix together hot pepper sauce, sugar, allspice, garlic, coriander and lime juice. Cut fish into cubes and add to the bowl. Stir to coat in the marinade, cover and leave in a cool place for 30 minutes. (See above.) Meanwhile, make the mango salsa. In a bowl, mix together mango, onion, chilli, coriander and lime rind and juice. Set aside. Remove the fish from the marinade, drain and arrange on a serving plate.

Heat the coconut milk and Scotch bonnet chilli in the fondue pot on top of the stove. Season with salt then transfer to the lighted spirit burner. Spear the fish on to the fondue forks and cook in the hot coconut milk for 2-3 minutes. Serve with the mango salsa.

Serves 4.

CRISPY COD BITES

700g (1½lb) thick cod fillet, skinned
seasoned flour, for dusting
2 eggs, beaten
115g (4oz/2 cups) fresh breadcrumbs
oil, for cooking
LEMON PARSLEY SAUCE:
25g (1oz/6 teaspoons) butter
6 teaspoons plain flour
225ml (8fl oz/1 cup) fish stock
grated rind and juice ½ lemon
1 tablespoon chopped fresh parsley
salt and freshly ground black pepper
3 tablespoons single cream

Cut fish in bite-sized pieces. Toss in flour, dip in egg, then coat in breadcrumbs.

To make lemon parsley sauce, melt butter in a saucepan, stir in flour and cook for 1 minute. Gradually add stock, then bring to the boil and simmer 1-2 minutes until sauce thickens, stirring all the time. Stir in lemon rind and juice, parsley and season with salt and pepper. Reheat for 1 minute, then stir in cream.

Heat the oil in the fondue pot on top of the stove then transfer to the lighted spirit burner. Spear the fish on to fondue forks and cook in the hot oil. Serve the fish with the sauce.

Serves 4-6.

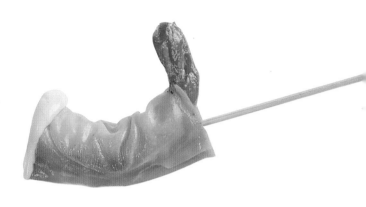

SEAFOOD KEBABS

8 large scallops
550g (1¼lb) monkfish, boned
seasoned flour, for dusting
oil, for cooking
TARRAGON WINE SAUCE:
25g (1oz/6 teaspoons) butter
1 shallot, finely chopped
150ml (5fl oz/⅔ cup) dry white wine
2 teaspoons chopped fresh tarragon
salt and freshly ground black pepper
4 tablespoons single cream

Remove the coral parts from scallops and reserve. Cut white parts in half.

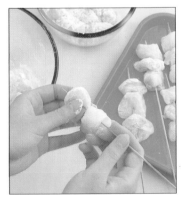

Cut monkfish into bite-sized pieces. Toss scallops and monkfish in seasoned flour. Thread one piece of scallop and 2 pieces of monkfish on to 16 bamboo skewers and keep in refrigerator until needed. Heat the oil in the fondue pot on top of the stove then transfer to lighted spirit burner.

To make sauce, melt butter in a saucepan. Add shallot and cook until soft, then add reserved scallop corals and cook over a gentle heat for 5 minutes. Pour in wine, add tarragon and season with salt and pepper. Simmer for 5 minutes. Purée sauce in a blender or food processor until smooth, then return to saucepan, stir in cream, and keep warm. Cook kebabs in hot oil until crisp and golden and serve with the sauce.

Serves 4.

PRAWNS IN JACKETS

2 sheets filo pastry approximately 45x25cm (18x10in)
25g (1oz/2 tablespoons) butter, melted
250g (9oz) (approximately 32) large raw prawns, peeled and thawed if frozen
salt and freshly ground black pepper
oil, for cooking
WASABI MAYONNAISE:
150ml (5fl oz/⅔ cup) mayonnaise
1 teaspoon wasabi paste
2 teaspoons lime juice

Make the wasabi mayonnaise. In a bowl, mix together mayonnaise, wasabi paste and lime juice. Set aside.

Lightly brush sheets of filo pastry with melted butter. Cut each sheet into strips across. The strips should be as wide as the prawns are long. Cut each strip in half across. Dry prawns on paper towels and season with salt and pepper. Roll a strip of pastry round each prawn and arrange on a serving dish.

Heat the oil in the fondue pot on top of the stove then transfer to the lighted spirit burner. Spear the wrapped prawns on the fondue forks and cook in the hot oil for 2 minutes or until crisp and golden. Serve with the wasabi mayonnaise.

Serves 4.

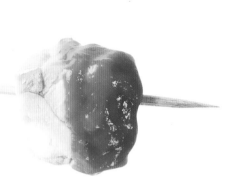

SEAFOOD FONDUE

225g (8oz) raw tiger prawns
550ml (20fl oz/2½ cups) good fish stock
½ lemon, sliced
1 small onion, peeled
225g (8oz) monkfish, skinned
225g (8oz) thick cod fillet, skinned
225g (8oz) scallops
lemon wedges and parsley sprigs, to garnish
Rouille (see page 88), to serve

Peel the prawns and place the shells in a saucepan with the stock, lemon and onion. Bring to the boil and simmer for 10 minutes.

Cut monkfish and cod into cubes and halve the scallops if they are large. Arrange on serving plates with the peeled prawns. Garnish with lemon wedges and parsley sprigs. Cover and keep cool.

Strain stock into the fondue pot, bring back to the boil on top of the stove then transfer to the lighted spirit burner. Spear the fish on to the fondue forks and cook in the hot stock for 2-3 minutes. Serve with Rouille.

Serves 6.

VARIATION: The selection of fish can be varied according to personal preference and what is available.

SWEET & SOUR FISH FONDUE

2 eggs
115g (4oz/1 cup) plain flour
700g (1½lb) boneless skinless firm white fish
   such as monkfish, cut into cubes
oil, for cooking
SWEET & SOUR SAUCE:
1 tablespoon oil
1 small onion, finely chopped
1 green pepper, seeded and sliced
1 teaspoon cornflour
2 tablespoons soft brown sugar
2 tablespoons white wine vinegar
2 tablespoons tomato purée
juice 1 small orange
2 tablespoons soy sauce
2 tablespoons finely chopped pineapple

To make sauce, heat oil in a saucepan. Add onion and cook for 5 minutes until beginning to soften. Add pepper and cook for 5 more minutes. In a small bowl, blend cornflour with 4 tablespoons water and add to the pan with sugar, vinegar, tomato purée, orange juice, soy sauce and pineapple. Bring to the boil, stirring, and cook until the sauce thickens. Keep warm.

Make the batter; whisk eggs with 200ml (7fl oz/scant 1 cup) iced water until frothy. Add flour and beat until just blended. Divide between 6 small bowls. Divide the fish between 6 serving plates. Heat oil in the fondue pot on top of the stove then transfer to the lighted spirit burner. Spear the fish on to the fondue forks, dip in the batter, then in hot oil for 2-3 minutes until batter is crisp and golden. Serve with the sweet and sour sauce.

Serves 6.

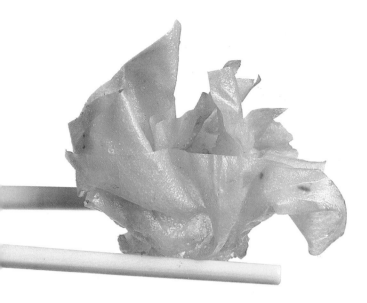

WAFER-WRAPPED PRAWNS

350g (12oz) peeled prawns, coarsely chopped
1 fresh green chilli, seeded and finely chopped
2 teaspoons oyster sauce
2 sheets filo pastry
oil, for cooking
CHILLI SAUCE:
4 tablespoons tomato ketchup
1-2 teaspoons chilli sauce
½ teaspoon sesame oil

In a bowl, mix prawns, chilli and oyster sauce together.

Cut filo pastry into 10cm (4in) squares. Place a heaped teaspoon of prawn filling in the centre of each square, then draw the corners of the pastry together and twist them to form little bundles. Place on a floured serving plate. Cover and chill until required. (Do not make these too far in advance – as bases become soggy if left to stand for too long.) Heat the oil in the fondue pot on top of the stove then transfer to the lighted spirit burner.

To make chilli sauce, put tomato ketchup, chilli sauce, 2 tablespoons water and sesame oil into a saucepan and heat gently for 3-4 minutes. Cook bundles using small Chinese wire strainers – this makes it easier and safer when lifting bundles out of the hot oil. Serve the prawn bundles with the hot chilli sauce, as a starter.

Makes 24.

PIRI PIRI PRAWNS

1 fresh red chilli, seeded and very finely chopped
½ teaspoon paprika
½ teaspoon ground coriander
1 clove garlic, crushed
finely grated rind 1 lime
salt and freshly ground black pepper
250g (9oz) large raw prawns, peeled and thawed if frozen
oil, for cooking
lime wedges, to garnish
Aioli (see page 89) and bread, to serve

In a bowl, mix together chilli, paprika, ground coriander, garlic, lime rind, salt and pepper.

Add prawns and mix well. Cover and leave in a cool place for 30 minutes. Heat the oil in the fondue pot on top of the stove then transfer to the lighted spirit burner.

Thread prawns on to fondue forks or bamboo skewers and cook in the hot oil for 1 minute or until pink. Serve, garnished with lime wedges, with the aioli and bread.

Serves 4.

ANCHOVY & PRAWN FONDUE

50g (2oz) anchovy fillets, drained
1 clove garlic, halved
150ml (5fl oz/⅔ cup) dry white wine
115g (4oz/1 cup) grated Gruyère cheese
225g (8oz/2 cups) grated Cheddar cheese
1 teaspoon cornflour
2 tablespoons dry sherry
Tabasco sauce
TO SERVE:
225g (8oz) large peeled cooked prawns
cubes of French bread

Place anchovy fillets in a mortar and pestle and pound to a paste. Arrange prawns and bread on serving plates.

Rub inside of a fondue pot with cut clove of garlic. Pour in wine and heat gently on the stove until bubbling. Gradually stir in cheeses. Heat gently, stirring, until the cheese has melted. In a small bowl, blend cornflour with the sherry.

Stir cornflour mixture into cheese and add Tabasco sauce, to taste, and anchovy paste. Cook gently, stirring until thick and creamy. Transfer pot to the lighted spirit burner. Serve with the prawns and bread.

Serves 4-6.

Note: Alternatively serve with Devilled Sauce (see page 47).

SPICY PRAWNS

700g (1½lb) cooked Mediterranean prawns
2 tablespoons oil
1 teaspoon paprika
2 tablespoons lemon juice
oil, for cooking
PIQUANT SAUCE:
300ml (10fl oz/1¼ cups) tomato juice
2 teaspoons demerara sugar
2 teaspoons red wine vinegar
¼ teaspoon ground cinnamon
¼ teaspoon ground ginger
1 small fresh red chilli, seeded and finely chopped

Peel prawns, leaving tail shells on, if desired, and put into a bowl. Add oil, paprika and lemon juice; mix well.

Cover prawns and leave to marinate for at least 1 hour in refrigerator. To make piquant sauce, put all ingredients into a saucepan and simmer for 15 minutes. Keep warm.

Drain and arrange prawns on a serving plate. Heat the oil in the fondue pot on top of the stove then transfer to the lighted spirit burner. Heat the prawns in the hot oil and serve with hot piquant sauce.

Serves 6 as a starter, 4 as a main course.

Note: Raw Mediterranean prawns may be used, if desired. Follow instructions given above, then cook raw prawns in hot oil for 2-3 minutes.

BAGNA CAUDA

50g (2oz/¼ cup) butter
4 cloves garlic, crushed
50g (2oz) can anchovy fillets, drained and roughly
  chopped
150ml (5fl oz/⅔ cup) mild extra virgin olive oil
TO SERVE:
a selection of raw and blanched vegetables such as
  celery, carrots, fennel, peppers, radishes, asparagus,
  cauliflower, baby artichoke hearts
hard boiled quails' eggs
breadsticks
toasted cubes of ciabatta bread

Arrange vegetables, eggs and bread on serving plates.

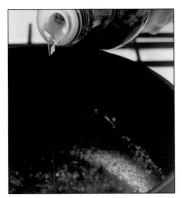

Gently heat butter in a heavy saucepan. Add garlic and cook gently, for 2 minutes. Add anchovies, then pour in oil very slowly, stirring constantly. Cook gently, stirring, for about 10 minutes. Do not allow to boil. The sauce in ready when anchovies have become a paste.

Transfer sauce to an earthenware bagna cauda pot or a fondue pot and place over the lighted spirit burner. To serve, dip vegetables, eggs and bread into the anchovy sauce.

Serves 4-6.

CRISPY CRUMBED MUSSELS

1kg (2¼lb) fresh mussels in shells
2 lemons, quartered
6 cloves garlic, peeled
2 eggs, beaten
115g (4oz/2 cups) fresh breadcrumbs
oil, for cooking
lemon wedges, to garnish
Rouille (see page 88), to serve

Scrub mussels and remove the beards. Discard any which do not close when tapped sharply. Place mussels in a large pan with lemon quarters and garlic. Add 4 tablespoons of water to the pan.

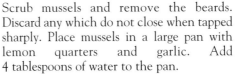

Cover and cook on a high heat for a few minutes, shaking pan occasionally until mussels open. Discard any which remain closed. Drain mussels and remove from shells. Dry on paper towels. Place beaten egg and breadcrumbs in 2 separate shallow dishes. Dip the mussels into egg, allowing the excess to drip back, then dip in breadcrumbs. Place on a serving dish.

Heat the oil in the fondue pot on top of the stove then transfer to the lighted spirit burner. Thread the mussels, two at a time, on to fondue forks or bamboo skewers and cook in the hot oil for 1 minute or until crisp and golden. Serve, garnished with lemon wedges, with the rouille.

Serves 4.

VARIATION: For a quick version of this dish, ready prepared breaded mussels, squid or scampi could be used.

THAI FISH CAKES

450g (1lb) boneless cod fillet
2 tablespoons chopped fresh coriander
1 tablespoon Thai red curry paste
1 small egg, beaten
1 teaspoon light muscovado sugar
1 tablespoon cornflour
1 teaspoon salt
oil, for cooking
lime wedges, to garnish
CHILLI DIPPING SAUCE:
4 tablespoons rice vinegar
4 tablespoons soy sauce
1 teaspoon light muscovado sugar
1 clove garlic, crushed
1 fresh red chilli, seeded and finely chopped
1 teaspoon sesame oil

Cut cod into chunks and chop roughly in a food processor. Add chopped coriander, curry paste, egg, sugar, cornflour and salt. Process again until well blended. Chill the mixture for 30 minutes. Divide mixture into 16 pieces, roll each into a ball then flatten slightly into a cake. Place on a serving dish and chill. (See above.) Make the dipping sauce. Place vinegar, soy sauce, sugar, garlic, chilli and sesame oil in a bowl and whisk together. Divide between small serving bowls.

Heat oil in the fondue pot on top of the stove then transfer to the lighted spirit burner. To cook the fishcakes, place them in wire baskets and dip into hot oil for 2-3 minutes until golden and cooked through. Serve, garnished with lime wedges, with the dipping sauce.

Serves 4.

SWORDFISH ACAPULCO

700g (1½lb) swordfish steaks, cut into bite-size pieces
MARINADE:
4 tablespoons oil
150ml (5fl oz/⅔ cup) dry white wine
1 clove garlic, crushed
THOUSAND ISLAND SAUCE:
1 hard boiled egg
225ml (8fl oz/1 cup) mayonnaise
1 teaspoon tomato purée
2 tablespoons chopped stuffed olives
2 tablespoons finely chopped onion
salt and freshly ground black pepper
1 tablespoon chopped fresh parsley

Combine marinade ingredients; stir in fish.

Cover and leave fish to marinate in refrigerator for 2-3 hours. To make Thousand Island sauce, chop hard boiled egg. Put all ingredients into a bowl, season to taste with salt and pepper and mix together. Spoon into a serving dish.

Drain the fish from the marinade and arrange in a serving dish. Heat the oil in the fondue pot on top of the stove then transfer to the lighted spirit burner. Cook the fish in the oil and serve with the Thousand Island sauce.

Serves 4.

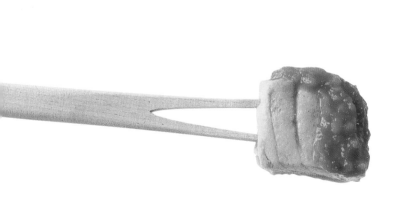

NIÇOISE FONDUE

MARRAKESH SWORDFISH FONDUE

1 tablespoon olive oil
1 onion, finely chopped
2 cloves garlic, crushed
400g (14oz) can chopped tomatoes
115ml (4fl oz/½ cup) dry white wine
1 teaspoon dried herbes de Provence
100g (3½oz) canned or bottled anchovies, drained
25g (1oz/2 tablespoons) pitted olives, chopped
salt and freshly ground black pepper
350g (12oz) cooked French beans, halved
3 hard boiled eggs, quartered
4 tablespoons vinaigrette dressing
450g (1lb) fresh tuna fish
French bread, to serve

1 small red onion, finely chopped
2 cloves garlic, crushed
1 fresh red chilli, seeded and finely chopped
2 tablespoons chopped fresh coriander
1 tablespoon chopped fresh mint
1 teaspoon ground cumin
1 teaspoon paprika
pinch saffron strands
4 tablespoons olive oil
juice 1 lemon
salt
700g (1½lb) swordfish, skinned
oil, for cooking
green salad and warm pitta bread, to serve

Heat the oil in a pan, add onion and garlic and cook gently for 10 minutes or until soft. Add tomatoes, white wine, 70ml (2½fl oz/ ⅓ cup) water and herbes de Provence and simmer gently for about 10 minutes until well blended. (See above.) Process in a blender or food processor to make a smooth sauce then add anchovies and olives and process briefly until finely chopped. Season with salt and pepper and pour into the fondue pot.

In a bowl, mix together the onion, garlic, chilli, coriander, mint, cumin, paprika, saffron, olive oil, lemon juice and season with salt. (See above.) Cut monkfish into cubes. Add them to spice mixture in the bowl. Mix well to coat, cover and leave in a cool place for 1 hour.

Combine beans and eggs with vinaigrette dressing and place in a serving dish. Cut tuna fish into cubes and arrange on a serving dish. Heat tomato sauce on top of the stove until simmering then transfer to the lighted spirit burner. Spear cubes of tuna fish on fondue forks and cook in the hot tomato sauce for 2 minutes or until cooked as desired. Serve with the bean and egg salad and French bread.

Serves 4.

Using a slotted spoon, remove fish from the bowl and arrange on a serving plate. Heat oil in the fondue pot on top of the stove then transfer to the lighted spirit burner. Spear fish on to the fondue forks and cook in the hot oil for 2-3 minutes. Serve with salad and warm pitta bread.

Serves 4.

GEFILTE FISH

700g (1½lb) mixed white fish, skinned
1 small onion, quartered
1 egg, beaten
2 tablespoons chopped fresh parsley
25g (1oz/¼ cup) ground almonds
4 tablespoons fine matzo meal
salt and freshly ground black pepper
oil, for cooking
CREAMY BEETROOT SAUCE:
150ml (5fl oz/⅔ cup) thick sour cream
50g (2oz) cooked beetroot, grated
1 tablespoon horseradish sauce

Coarsely mince the fish and onion or chop in a food processor.

Add the remaining ingredients except the oil to minced fish and mix well. (The mixture should be stiff; if necessary add a little more matzo meal.) With wetted hands, form mixture into 36 smooth balls. Place on a tray and refrigerate for at least 30 minutes. Heat oil in the fondue pot on top of the stove then transfer to the lighted spirit burner.

To make creamy beetroot sauce, put cream into a bowl, add grated beetroot, then mix in horseradish sauce and season with salt and pepper. Cook the gefilte fish in the hot oil and serve with the sauce.

Serves 6.

SMOKED FISH GOUJONS

4 heaped tablespoons plain flour
salt and freshly ground black pepper
700g (1½lb) skinless and boneless smoked fish
   fillets
3 eggs, beaten
115g (4oz/2 cups) fresh breadcrumbs
oil, for cooking
lemon wedges, to garnish
REMOULADE SAUCE:
150ml (5fl oz/⅔ cup) mayonnaise
1 teaspoon Dijon mustard
2 teaspoons finely chopped capers
2 teaspoons finely chopped gherkins
2 teaspoons finely chopped fresh tarragon

To make the sauce mix together the mayonnaise, mustard, capers, gherkins and tarragon. Set aside. (See above.) Place flour in a shallow dish. Season with salt and pepper and mix together. Cut fish into strips about 1cm (½in) wide. Dust strips with seasoned flour. Place beaten egg and breadcrumbs in 2 separate shallow dishes. Dip each piece of fish in the egg allowing the excess to drip back in then dip in breadcrumbs. Place on a serving dish.

Heat oil in the fondue pot on top of the stove then transfer to the lighted spirit burner. Spear fish on to fondue forks and cook in oil for 1-2 minutes until crisp and golden. Serve, garnished with lemon wedges, with the sauce.

Serves 4.

AMANDINE TROUT

4 trout
seasoned flour, for dusting
2 eggs, beaten
225g (8oz/2 cups) blanched almonds, lightly toasted
   and finely chopped
oil, for cooking
DILL SAUCE:
4 teaspoons cornflour
150ml (5fl oz/⅔ cup) fish stock
150ml (5fl oz/⅔ cup) milk
2 tablespoons chopped fresh dill
salt and freshly ground black pepper

Clean and bone the fish and cut off fins, then slice into pieces just under 1cm (½in) thick.

Toss pieces of trout first in seasoned flour, then dip in egg and finally coat in chopped almonds. Place on a serving plate and refrigerate until ready to cook. Heat oil in the fondue pot on top of the stove then transfer to the lighted spirit burner.

To make dill sauce, in a saucepan blend cornflour smoothly with a little fish stock, then add remainder together with the milk and heat until simmering, stirring all the time. Cook for 2 minutes until thickened. Stir in dill and season with salt and pepper. Cook the fish in the hot oil and serve with the hot dill sauce.

Serves 4.

FISH FIREPOT

700g (1½lb) assorted boneless skinless fish such as
   salmon, cod and monkfish
225g (8oz) large raw peeled prawns or scallops or a
   mixture of both
450g (1lb) pak choi, cut into thin strips
225g (8oz) button mushrooms, halved
200g (7oz) fine egg noodles, cooked
chopped fresh coriander
1.75 litres (60fl oz/7½ cups) fish stock
3 tablespoons rice wine or dry sherry
1 teaspoon salt
DIPPING SAUCE:
1 fresh red chilli, seeded and finely chopped
2 cloves garlic, crushed
4 tablespoons soy sauce
1 tablespoon tamarind paste

Cut fish into thin slices and halve scallops if they are large. (See above.) Arrange fish on 4 or 6 individual serving plates. Cover and chill until required. Arrange pak choi, mushrooms and noodles on serving plates. Place chopped coriander in a shallow dish. Make dipping sauce. In a bowl, mix together chilli, garlic, soy sauce and tamarind paste. If using a Mongolian hotpot, light it and place on the table. Pour in stock and add rice wine or sherry and salt. Bring to the boil.

(If using a fondue pot, pour stock and rice wine or sherry into the pot, add salt and bring to the boil on the stove. Transfer to the lighted spirit burner.) Dip pieces of fish into stock, using chopsticks or Chinese wire strainers. Remove from stock and dip into sauce or coriander before eating. From time to time add mushrooms and pak choi to the stock, and when cooked remove and eat. Finally, add noodles to stock to heat through, then serve the soup in warmed bowls.

Serves 4-6.

MANHATTAN FONDUE

8-10 bagels
115g (4oz) smoked salmon
400g (14oz/1¾ cups) cream cheese
175ml (6fl oz/¾ cup) milk
1 tablespoon chopped fresh dill
salt and freshly ground black pepper

Split the bagels, toast lightly and cut into bite sized pieces. Divide between 4-6 serving plates.

Chop smoked salmon into small pieces. Place cream cheese and milk in the fondue pot and heat gently on the stove until cheese has melted to a smooth sauce.

Stir in the dill and smoked salmon and season with salt and a generous amount of black pepper. Transfer the pot to the lighted spirit burner and keep warm over a low heat. Spear the pieces of bagel on fondue forks and dip into the sauce.

Serves 4-6.

SEAFOOD TEMPURA

4 plaice fillets, skinned
225g (8oz) halibut, skinned and boned
225g (8oz) fresh salmon, skinned and boned
225g (8oz) scampi tails, thawed if frozen
4 small squid, cut into rings
1 quantity Chilli Sauce (see page 31)
3 teaspoons peeled and grated fresh root ginger and
   225g (8oz) daikon, grated, to garnish
1 quantity Batter (see page 62)
oil, for cooking

Cut plaice, halibut and salmon into thin slices or fingers; arrange on a platter with scampi and squid.

Make chilli sauce. Prepare the garnish by mixing ginger and daikon together.

Make the batter. Heat oil in the fondue pot on top of the stove then transfer to the lighted spirit burner. Each person spears a piece of fish, dips it into the batter, then cooks it in the hot oil. The cooked food is then dipped into the chilli sauce and eaten with the garnish.

Serves 4-6.

MEAT
& POULTRY

STEAK BOURGUIGNONNE

1kg (2¼lb) lean fillet or rump steak
oil, for cooking
small baked potatoes and green salad, to serve
  (optional)
FOUR SAUCES:
550ml (20fl oz/2½ cups) mayonnaise
50g (2oz) anchovies, drained
2 tablespoons horseradish sauce
2 tablespoons tomato purée
2 teaspoons hot pepper sauce
1 tablespoon curry paste

Cut steak into 2.5cm (1in) cubes and arrange on 4-6 serving plates.

To make the sauces, divide mayonnaise between 4 bowls. In a mortar and pestle, pound anchovies to a purée and stir into one of the bowls of mayonnaise. Stir horseradish sauce into another, tomato purée and hot pepper sauce into another and curry paste into the last bowl. Transfer sauces to small serving bowls.

Heat oil in the fondue pot on top of the stove then transfer to the lighted spirit burner. Spear steak on to fondue forks and cook in hot oil according to individual taste. Serve with the sauces, and baked potatoes and salad, if you like.

Serves 6.

VARIATIONS: Lean fillet of lamb could be served instead of or as well as the steak.

MEXICAN FONDUE

1kg (2¼lb) lean rump steak
oil, for cooking
MEXICAN SAUCE:
1 tablespoon oil
½ Spanish onion, finely chopped
1 clove garlic, crushed
400g (14oz) can tomatoes
2 tablespoons tomato purée
½ teaspoon chilli powder
1 fresh green chilli, seeded and finely chopped
salt and freshly ground black pepper

Cut meat into 2.5cm (1in) cubes and arrange on a serving plate.

To make Mexican sauce, heat oil in a saucepan, add onion and garlic and cook gently until softened. Stir in tomatoes and their juice, tomato purée and chilli powder. Simmer, uncovered, for 10 minutes.

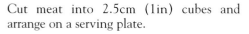

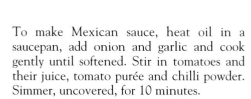

Remove sauce from heat and purée in a blender or food processor until smooth, or press through a sieve to give a smooth sauce. Return to the heat, add chopped chilli and simmer for a further 15 minutes. Season with salt and pepper. Heat oil in the fondue pot on top of the stove then transfer to the lighted spirit burner. Cook the meat in the hot oil and serve with the sauce.

Serves 4-6.

FONDUE BOURGUIGNONNE

1kg (2¼lb) fillet steak
oil, for cooking
TOMATO SAUCE:
1 tablespoon oil
2 shallots, finely chopped
1 clove garlic, crushed
400g (14oz) can chopped tomatoes
2 tablespoons tomato purée
salt and freshly ground black pepper
1 tablespoon chopped fresh parsley

To make tomato sauce, heat oil in a saucepan, add shallots and cook gently until soft.

Stir in garlic, tomatoes with their juice and tomato purée. Season with salt and pepper, bring to the boil, then reduce heat and simmer, uncovered, for about 30 minutes or until sauce has reduced and thickened. Stir in parsley and serve hot or cold.

Cut the steak into 2.5cm (1in) cubes and put into a serving dish. Heat oil in the fondue pot on top of the stove then transfer to the lighted spirit burner. Each person spears a cube of meat with a fondue fork and immerses the meat in the hot oil to fry. The meat cube is cooked according to individual taste.

Serves 4-6.

Note: Serve also with Garlic Sauce (see page 60) and Cool Curry Dip (see page 63).

CAJUN MEATBALLS

1 tablespoon oil
1 onion, finely chopped
1 teaspoon coriander seeds
½ teaspoon cardamom seeds
450g (1lb) lean minced steak
50g (2oz/1 cup) fresh breadcrumbs
1 small egg, beaten
grated rind ½ lemon
¼-½ teaspoon chilli powder
2 tablespoons chopped fresh coriander
salt and freshly ground black pepper
oil, for cooking
TO SERVE:
Chilli Tomato Sauce (see page 88)
pitta bread
shredded lettuce

Heat oil in a saucepan. Add onion and cook for 10 minutes until soft. Set aside to cool. In a small heavy based saucepan, dry fry coriander and cardamom seeds for a few minutes until golden, then crush, using a mortar and pestle. In a bowl, mix together the onion, minced steak, crushed spices, breadcrumbs, egg, lemon rind, chilli powder, coriander, and salt and pepper until thoroughly combined.

Form the mixture into walnut sized balls. Arrange on serving plates and chill until required. Heat oil in the fondue pot on top of the stove then transfer to the lighted spirit burner. Spear meatballs on to the fondue forks and cook in the hot oil for 3-4 minutes until cooked. Serve with the sauce, pitta bread and lettuce.

Serves 4-6.

PROVENÇAL BEEF

2 cloves garlic, crushed
150ml (5fl oz/²⁄₃ cup) red wine
grated rind and juice ½ orange
1 tablespoon chopped fresh rosemary
1 teaspoon dried herbes de provence
2 tablespoons olive oil
550g (1¼lb) rump or fillet steak
salt and freshly ground black pepper
oil, for cooking
TOMATO SALAD:
450g (1lb) tomatoes, sliced
6 spring onions, thinly sliced
2 tablespoons shredded basil leaves
1 clove garlic, crushed
6 tablespoons olive oil
2 tablespoons balsamic vinegar

In a bowl, mix together garlic, wine, orange rind and juice, rosemary, herbes de provence and olive oil. Cut beef into 2.5cm (1in) cubes and add to marinade. Cover and marinate overnight in the refrigerator. Meanwhile, make salad. Arrange sliced tomatoes on individual serving plates. Sprinkle spring onions and basil over tomatoes. In a small bowl, whisk together garlic, olive oil, balsamic vinegar, salt and pepper. Pour over tomatoes, cover and leave to marinate for 1 hour.

Remove beef from marinade and dry on paper towels. Season with salt and pepper and arrange on serving plates. Heat oil in the fondue pot on top of the stove then transfer to the lighted spirit burner. Spear the beef on to fondue forks and cook in hot oil for 3-4 minutes until cooked. Serve with the tomato salad.

Serves 4.

TERIYAKI FONDUE

1kg (2¼lb) fillet steak
3 teaspoons light soft brown sugar
115ml (4fl oz/½ cup) soy sauce
6 tablespoons dry sherry
2 cloves garlic, crushed
1 teaspoon ground ginger
oil, for cooking
BEANSPROUT SALAD:
1 small head Chinese leaves
225g (8oz) fresh beansprouts
1 red pepper, seeded and finely sliced
½ bunch spring onions, shredded
6 tablespoons sunflower oil
1 tablespoon wine vinegar

Thinly cut steak into long narrow strips.

Put 1 teaspoon of sugar and 2 tablespoons of soy sauce into a bowl and set aside. In a large bowl, combine remaining sugar and soy sauce, sherry, garlic and ginger. Add strips of meat and leave to marinate for 1 hour. Weave the strips of meat on to 20-24 bamboo skewers ready for cooking.

Heat oil in the fondue pot on top of the stove then transfer to the lighted spirit burner. To prepare the salad, shred Chinese leaves and put into a bowl with beansprouts, pepper and spring onions. Add oil to reserved sugar and soy sauce, then whisk in vinegar and pour over salad. Toss lightly together. Cook the meat in hot oil and serve with the salad.

Serves 4-6.

TERIYAKI STEAK

700g (1½lb) fillet steak
5cm (2in) piece fresh root ginger
1 tablespoon oil
1 clove garlic, crushed
4 tablespoons soy sauce
2 tablespoons mirin or medium sherry
1 teaspoon soft light brown sugar
freshly ground black pepper
TO SERVE:
1 daikon radish
2 tablespoons wasabi paste
coriander sprigs

CHEESY MEATBALL FONDUE

700g (1½lb) lean minced beef
1 tablespoon finely chopped onion
25g (1oz/½ cup) fresh whole breadcrumbs
salt and freshly ground black pepper
115g (4oz) Cheddar cheese, diced
oil, for cooking
TANGY SAUCE:
1 tablespoon tomato purée
1 tablespoon red wine vinegar
2 tablespoons honey
2 teaspoons dry mustard
1 tablespoon Worcestershire sauce
300ml (10fl oz/1¼ cups) chicken stock
2 teaspoons cornflour
juice 1 orange

Cut the steaks into thin strips 1cm (½in) wide and 10cm (4in) long.

Mix together beef, onion and breadcrumbs. (See above.) Season meat mixture with salt and pepper and divide into 30 balls. Flatten each ball out, place a piece of cheese in centre, then mould meat around cheese, sealing it well to enclose cheese completely.

Peel ginger and grate into a bowl. Squeeze out liquid and put 1 tablespoon in a dish with oil, garlic, soy sauce, mirin or sherry and sugar. Add steak, mix well, cover and leave to marinate in the fridge for 1 hour. Meanwhile, prepare garnish. Peel daikon radish and grate into a bowl. Squeeze out as much liquid as possible and divide the grated radish between 4 serving plates. Place a little wasabi paste and a sprig of coriander on each plate.

Remove steak from marinade and pat dry with paper towels. Season with pepper. Thread strips of steak on to bamboo skewers and divide between 4 serving dishes. Heat oil in the fondue pot on top of the stove then transfer to the lighted spirit burner. Cook the steak in hot oil for 2-3 minutes until cooked. Serve with daikon radish and wasabi, garnished with coriander.

Serves 4.

To make sauce, put tomato purée, wine vinegar, honey, mustard, Worcestershire sauce and stock into a saucepan and simmer for 10 minutes. Blend cornflour smoothly with orange juice, then stir into the sauce and simmer for 1 minute, stirring all the time. Heat oil in the fondue pot on top of the stove then transfer to the lighted spirit burner. Cook meatballs in the hot oil and serve with the sauce.

Serves 6.

VEAL MILANESE

700g (1½lb) leg veal, cubed
3 tablespoons seasoned plain flour
3 eggs, beaten
115g (4oz/1 cup) dry breadcrumbs
2 teaspoons finely grated lemon rind
oil, for cooking
ITALIAN SAUCE:
2 tablespoons olive oil
1 onion, finely chopped
1-2 cloves garlic, crushed
700g (1½lb) ripe tomatoes, peeled and chopped
5 tablespoons dry white wine
salt and freshly ground black pepper
1 tablespoon chopped fresh basil

Toss veal in flour; dip in egg and coat in mixed crumbs and lemon rind. (See above.) To make Italian sauce, heat oil in a saucepan, add onion and garlic and cook over a low heat until soft. Add tomatoes and wine and season with salt and pepper. Simmer for 30 minutes. Purée sauce in a blender or food processor until smooth, or press through a sieve.

Heat oil in the fondue pot on top of the stove then transfer to the lighted spirit burner. Stir basil into sauce and reheat sauce. Cook meat in hot and oil and serve with sauce.

Serves 4-6.

Note: Serve also with Lemon Parsley Sauce (see page 28), omitting fish stock and using chicken stock instead.

MEXICAN BEEF & GUACAMOLE

700g (1½lb) sirloin or rump steak
2 teaspoons chilli sauce
2 cloves garlic, crushed
1 tablespoon chopped fresh coriander
1 teaspoon each dried oregano and ground cumin
juice 1 lime
oil, for cooking
tortilla chips, to serve
GUACAMOLE:
2-3 ripe avocados, depending on the size
½ red onion, finely chopped
1 tablespoon chopped fresh coriander
1 clove garlic, crushed
1 red chilli, seeded and finely chopped
2 tomatoes, peeled, seeded and finely chopped
juice ½-1 lime
pinch sugar
salt and freshly ground black pepper

Cut steak into 2.5cm (1in) cubes. In a bowl, mix together chilli sauce, garlic, coriander, oregano, cumin and lime juice. Add steak and mix well. (See above.) Cover and set aside in the fridge for 1-2 hours. Meanwhile, make guacamole. Peel and stone avocados, place in a bowl and mash with a fork. Do not make mixture too smooth. Stir in onion, coriander, garlic, chilli and tomato. Then stir in lime juice, sugar, salt and pepper to taste.

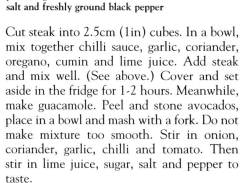

Leave to stand for 30 minutes, but no longer than 1 hour. Just before serving, stir again and transfer to small serving bowls. Remove steak from marinade, dry with paper towels and arrange on serving plates. Heat oil in the fondue pot on top of the stove then transfer to the lighted spirit burner. Spear cubes of steak on to fondue forks and cook in hot oil for 3-4 minutes until cooked. Serve with guacamole and tortilla chips.

Serves 4-6.

KOFTAS & RAITA

1 small onion, roughly chopped
1 clove garlic, chopped
2.5cm (1in) piece fresh root ginger, peeled and chopped
1 teaspoon ground cumin
1 teaspoon ground coriander
1 tablespoon oil
450g (1lb) lean minced lamb
3 tablespoons chopped fresh coriander
salt and freshly ground black pepper
1 small egg, beaten
oil, for cooking
naan bread or chapatis, to serve
RAITA:
½ cucumber
300ml (10fl oz/1½ cups) Greek yogurt
3 tablespoons chopped fresh mint

PROVENÇAL MEATBALLS

700g (1½lb) minced beef
1 small onion, finely chopped
50g (2oz) stuffed olives, finely chopped
1 small egg, beaten
salt and freshly ground black pepper
plain flour, for coating
oil, for cooking
PROVENÇAL DIP:
1 aubergine, diced
3 tablespoons olive oil
1 shallot, finely chopped
1 clove garlic, crushed
450g (1lb) tomatoes, peeled and chopped
1 tablespoon tomato purée
1 tablespoon chopped fresh parsley

Put onion, garlic and ginger in a blender or food processor and chop finely, without turning to a paste. Add cumin and ground coriander and process briefly to blend. Heat oil in a frying pan, add onion mixture and cook for 2-3 minutes, stirring. (See above.) Leave to cool. In a bowl, mix together minced lamb, coriander, seasoning and cooled onion mixture. Mix thoroughly. Add just enough beaten egg to bind mixture together. With floured hands, roll mixture into bite sized balls. Arrange on serving plates and chill until required.

Sprinkle aubergine for dip with salt and drain for 30 minutes. In a bowl, mix together ingredients for meatballs, except flour. With wetted hands, roll mixture into 36 small balls, then coat in flour. Chill in refrigerator until needed.

To make the raita, grate cucumber coarsely. Squeeze out as much liquid as possible then mix cucumber, yogurt and mint together. Season with salt and pepper and transfer to small serving bowls. Heat oil in the fondue pot on top of the stove then transfer to the lighted spirit burner. Spear the koftas on to fondue forks and cook in the hot oil for 3-4 minutes until cooked. Serve with the raita and naan bread or chapatis.

Serves 4-6.

To make dip, rinse aubergine and pat dry. Heat oil in a large saucepan and cook shallot and garlic gently for 2 minutes. Add aubergine and cook gently for 10 minutes. Add tomatoes and purée, cover and cook for a further 5-8 minutes until vegetables are almost reduced to a pulp. Stir in parsley and seasoning. Heat oil in the fondue pot on top of the stove then transfer to the lighted spirit burner. Cook the meatballs in oil and serve with the warm dip.

Serves 6.

MIDDLE EASTERN FONDUE

700g (1½lb) lean leg of lamb, cubed
MARINADE:
3 tablespoons olive oil
1 tablespoon lemon juice
1 clove garlic, crushed
1 tablespoon chopped fresh mint
1 teaspoon ground cinnamon
salt and freshly ground black pepper
APRICOT SAUCE:
1 tablespoon oil
1 shallot, finely chopped
400g (14oz) can apricots in natural juice
1 tablespoon chopped fresh parsley

Mix marinade ingredients together and pour over cubed lamb.

Cover lamb mixture and leave to marinate for at least 2 hours, or preferably overnight. To make apricot sauce, heat oil in a saucepan, add shallot and cook over a low heat until soft. Add apricots and the juice and simmer for 5 minutes.

Purée sauce in a blender or food processor, then season with salt and pepper and stir in parsley. Reheat before serving. Remove lamb from marinade and arrange on a serving plate. Heat the oil in the fondue pot on top of the stove then transfer to the lighted spirit burner. Cook the lamb in the oil and serve with the sauce.

Serves 4.

TURKISH LAMB

700g (1½lb) lean lamb
2 cloves garlic, crushed
4 tablespoons lemon juice
pinch chilli powder
1 teaspoon ground cumin
1 teaspoon ground coriander
½ teaspoon ground cinnamon
salt and freshly ground black pepper
oil, for cooking
TO SERVE:
Tomato and Olive Salsa (see page 90)
pitta bread

Cut the lamb into 2.5cm (1in) cubes.

Crush garlic and place in a bowl. Add lemon juice, chilli powder, cumin, ground coriander and cinnamon, and stir. Add lamb and mix until well coated with marinade. Cover and leave to marinate in a cool place for 2 hours.

Remove lamb from marinade and pat dry with paper towels. Season with salt and pepper. Arrange the lamb on 4 serving plates. Heat the oil in the fondue pot on top of the stove then transfer to the lighted spirit burner. Spear the lamb on to fondue forks and cook in the hot oil for 3-4 minutes until cooked. Serve with the tomato and olive salsa.

Serves 4.

MINCED LAMB FONDUE

550g (1¼lb) minced lean lamb
3 spring onions, finely chopped
50g (2oz/1 cup) fresh breadcrumbs
2 tablespoons chopped fresh parsley
salt and freshly ground black pepper
oil, for cooking
MUSHROOM SAUCE:
50g (2oz/¼ cup) butter
175g (6oz) mushrooms, finely chopped
6 teaspoons plain flour
300ml (10fl oz/1¼ cups) milk
1 tablespoon dry sherry

Put the ingredients for lamb balls into a bowl.
Season with salt and pepper and mix well.

With wetted hands, shape mixture into 20-
24 balls, the size of a walnut, and place on a
serving plate. Heat the oil in the fondue pot
on top of the stove then transfer to the
lighted spirit burner.

To make sauce, melt butter in a saucepan,
add mushrooms and cook gently for
5 minutes. Stir in flour, then slowly add milk
and bring to the boil, stirring. Simmer for a
further 5 minutes, then season with salt and
pepper and add sherry. Cook the lamb balls
in the hot oil and serve with the warm sauce.

Serves 4-6.

Note: Serve also with Devilled Sauce (see
right).

BACON PARCELS

350g (12oz) streaky bacon, rinds removed
225g (8oz) chicken livers
oil, for cooking
DEVILLED SAUCE:
15g (½oz) butter
1 shallot, finely chopped
3 teaspoons plain flour
150ml (5fl oz/⅔ cup) chicken stock
4 tomatoes, peeled and chopped
1 tablespoon tomato purée
2 teaspoons sugar
1 tablespoon red wine vinegar
3 teaspoons Worcestershire sauce
½ teaspoon paprika
pinch cayenne pepper

Cut rashers in half; cut livers into pieces.
(See above.) Wrap bacon around chicken
livers and spear on to bamboo skewers. Place
on a serving plate. Heat the oil in the fondue
pot on top of the stove then transfer to the
lighted spirit burner.

To make devilled sauce, melt butter in a
saucepan, add shallot and cook until soft.
Stir in flour, then add stock and remaining
ingredients. Simmer for 15 minutes, then
strain sauce. Cook the bacon parcels in the
hot oil and serve with the hot sauce.

Serves 4.

Note: Serve also with Creamy Onion Sauce
(see page 62).

PORK SATAY

1 teaspoon tamarind paste
2 cloves garlic, crushed
2 tablespoons soy sauce
1 teaspoon ground cumin
1 teaspoon ground coriander
½ teaspoon chilli powder
salt
450g (1lb) lean pork steaks
oil, for cooking
SATAY SAUCE:
2 tablespoons smooth peanut butter
200ml (7fl oz/scant 1 cup) coconut cream
2 teaspoons red Thai curry paste
1 tablespoon fish sauce
1 tablespoon soft brown sugar

In a bowl mix together tamarind paste, garlic, soy sauce, ground cumin, ground coriander, chilli and salt. (See above.) Place pork steaks between 2 pieces of clear film and beat out flat with a meat hammer or rolling pin. Cut into strips then place in the bowl with marinade. Mix well then cover and leave in a cool place for 1 hour. Remove from marinade, dry with paper towels and thread on to bamboo skewers. Arrange on serving plates.

To make satay sauce, place peanut butter, coconut cream, red curry paste, fish sauce and brown sugar in a pan. Heat gently to form a smooth sauce, adding a little water if necessary. Keep warm. Heat oil in the fondue pot on top of the stove then transfer to the lighted spirit burner. Cook the skewers of pork in the hot oil for 3-4 minutes until cooked. Serve with the satay sauce.

Serves 4.

CRISPY SAUSAGE BITES

450g (1lb) pork sausagemeat
1 small onion, finely chopped
85g (3oz/⅓ cup) cream cheese
1 tablespoon chopped fresh parsley
1 teaspoon prepared mustard
25g (1oz/½ cup) fresh breadcrumbs
salt and freshly ground black pepper
2 eggs, beaten
85g (3oz/¾ cup) dry breadcrumbs
oil, for cooking
RELISH SAUCE:
Tomato Sauce (see page 41)
2 tablespoons sweet pickle relish

Put sausagemeat and onion into a frying pan; cook until lightly brown and crumbly.

Turn into a bowl and add cream cheese, parsley, mustard, fresh breadcrumbs and season with salt and pepper. Shape into 16-20 small firm balls, moulding to make them smooth. Dip first in beaten egg, then roll in dry breadcrumbs until evenly coated. Chill until required.

To make relish sauce, put tomato sauce in a saucepan, stir in relish and heat through. Keep warm. Heat oil in the fondue pot on top of the stove then transfer to the lighted spirit burner. Each person spears a sausage ball with a fondue fork and immerses it in the hot oil to fry until crisp and golden. Serve with the warm sauce.

Serves 4.

PORK & PEANUT SAUCE

½ teaspoon chilli powder
1 teaspoon ground coriander
½ teaspoon turmeric
3 teaspoons oil
3 teaspoons soy sauce
½ teaspoon salt
1kg (2¼lb) pork fillet, cubed
oil, for cooking
PEANUT SAUCE:
50g (2oz/⅔ cup) desiccated coconut
300ml (10fl oz/1¼ cups) boiling water
5 tablespoons crunchy peanut butter
2 teaspoons sugar
1 fresh green chilli, seeded and finely chopped
1 teaspoon lemon juice
1 clove garlic, crushed

In a bowl, mix together spices, oil, soy sauce and salt to make a paste. Add pork and with wet hands, knead paste into meat. Cover bowl and leave in the refrigerator for at least 2 hours.

To make peanut sauce, put coconut into a bowl, pour boiling water over and leave to stand for 15 minutes. Strain mixture into a saucepan, pressing well to extract all moisture. Discard coconut. Add remaining ingredients and mix well. Cook over a low heat, stirring until the sauce comes to the boil. Heat oil in the fondue pot on top of the stove then transfer to the lighted spirit burner. Cook the meat in hot oil and serve with the hot sauce.

Serves 4-6.

FIVE-SPICE DUCK

3-4 duck breasts, about 700g (1½lb) total weight
1 teaspoon sesame oil
3 tablespoons soy sauce
3 tablespoons rice wine or dry sherry
1 tablespoon honey
1 tablespoon lime juice
2 teaspoons five-spice powder
1 clove garlic, crushed
2.5cm (1in) piece fresh root ginger, grated
lime wedges, to garnish
oil, for cooking
TO SERVE:
shredded spring onions
shredded celery
hoisin or plum sauce
Chinese pancakes or flour tortillas

Remove skin and fat from duck breasts and cut meat into thin strips. Place in a shallow dish. In a bowl, mix together sesame oil, soy sauce, rice wine or sherry, honey, lime juice, five-spice powder, garlic and ginger. (See above.) Pour over duck and stir well. Cover and leave in a cool place to marinate for 30 minutes. Remove duck strips from marinade and dry on paper towels. Arrange on serving plates and garnish with lime wedges. Arrange spring onions and celery on serving plates and place hoisin or plum sauce in small bowls.

Warm Chinese pancakes or tortillas and keep warm. Heat oil in the fondue pot on top of the stove then transfer to the lighted spirit burner. Spear strips of duck on to fondue forks, or thread on to bamboo skewers. Cook in hot oil for 3-4 minutes until cooked. To serve, spread a little hoisin or plum sauce on a pancake or tortilla, add some spring onion and celery and place a few strips of cooked duck on top then roll up.

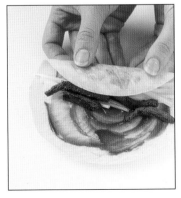

Serves 4-6.

FRUITY DUCK FONDUE

700g (1½lb) duck breast fillets, cut in pieces
6 teaspoons seasoned flour
1 teaspoon five-spice powder
oil, for cooking
MARMALADE SAUCE:
1 tablespoon demerara sugar
150ml (5fl oz/⅔ cup) orange juice
4 tablespoons mature orange marmalade
juice 1 lemon
50g (2oz/⅓ cup) raisins, chopped if large
WINE AND CHERRY SAUCE:
1 tablespoon sugar
350g (12oz) can black cherries, drained
85ml (3fl oz/⅓ cup) red wine
pinch mixed spice

Toss duck in flour and five-spice powder. (See above.) Place duck on a serving plate. To make marmalade sauce, put all the ingredients into a small saucepan and simmer for 5 minutes. Keep warm.

To make wine and cherry sauce. Put all ingredients into a saucepan and simmer for 15 minutes. Press through a sieve, discarding the stones. Keep warm. Heat oil in the fondue pot on top of the stove then transfer to the lighted spirit burner. Cook the duck in the hot oil and serve with the warm sauces.

Serves 4.

CURRIED APRICOT TURKEY

1 tablespoon oil
1 onion, finely chopped
1 clove garlic, crushed
2 bay leaves
juice 1 lemon
2 tablespoons curry powder
4 tablespoons apricot jam
4 tablespoons apple juice
salt
700g (1½lb) turkey fillet
4 tablespoons crème fraîche
oil, for cooking

Heat oil in a saucepan. Add onion, garlic and bay leaves and cook for 10 minutes until soft.

Add lemon juice, curry powder, apricot jam, apple juice and salt, to taste. Cook gently for 5 minutes. Transfer to a bowl and leave to cool. Cut turkey into 2.5cm (1in) cubes and add to cooled marinade. Mix well, cover and leave to marinate in the fridge for 2 hours.

Remove turkey and allow marinade to run back into the bowl. Dry turkey with paper towels and arrange on 4 serving plates. Transfer marinade to a pan and simmer for 2 minutes. Stir in crème fraîche. Heat oil in the fondue pot on top of the stove then transfer to the lighted spirit burner. Spear turkey on to fondue forks and cook in hot oil for 3-4 minutes until cooked. Serve with the sauce.

Serves 4.

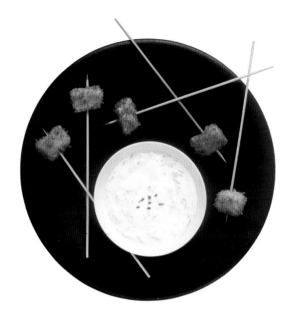

TURKEY NUGGETS

700g (1½lb) turkey fillets
3 tablespoons plain flour
salt and freshly ground black pepper
115g (4oz/1 cup) dry breadcrumbs
2 teaspoons finely grated lemon rind
2 large eggs, beaten
lemon wedges, to garnish
oil, for frying
HERB DIP:
200g (7oz) fromage frais
1 clove garlic, crushed
2 tablespoons chopped fresh tarragon
1 tablespoon chopped fresh chives
1 tablespoon chopped fresh chervil
salt and freshly ground black pepper

SPICY CHICKEN FONDUE

6 skinless, boneless chicken breasts
4 tablespoons oil
2 teaspoons paprika
½ teaspoon chilli powder
oil, for cooking
CURRY SAUCE:
1 tablespoon oil
1 onion, finely chopped
2 teaspoons mild curry powder
3 teaspoons plain flour
300ml (10fl oz/1¼ cups) milk
6 teaspoons mango chutney
salt and freshly ground black pepper

Cut chicken into 2cm (¾in) pieces and mix
with oil, paprika and chilli powder.

Place chicken on a serving plate. To make
curry sauce, heat oil in a saucepan, add
onion and cook until soft. Stir in curry
powder and cook for 2 minutes, then stir in
flour.

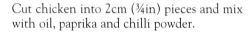

Cut turkey into bite sized cubes. In a bowl,
mix together flour, salt and pepper. In a
shallow dish, mix together breadcrumbs and
lemon rind. Pour beaten egg into another
shallow dish. Toss turkey cubes in seasoned
flour, dip in beaten egg then coat in
breadcrumbs. (See above.) Arrange on
serving plates and garnish with lemon
wedges. To make herb dip, place fromage
frais in a bowl, add garlic, tarragon, chives
and chervil and season with salt and pepper.
Mix well together then divide between small
serving bowls.

Heat oil in the fondue pot on top of the
stove then transfer to the lighted spirit
burner. Spear turkey nuggets on to fondue
forks and cook in hot oil for 3-4 minutes
until cooked. Serve with the herb dip.

Serves 4-6.

VARIATION: Chicken may be used as an
alternative to turkey.

Gradually stir in milk and bring slowly to the
boil, stirring all the time. Continue to cook
until sauce thickens. Simmer for 5 minutes,
then add chutney and season with salt and
pepper. Heat oil in the fondue pot on top of
the stove then transfer to the lighted spirit
burner. Cook the chicken in the hot oil and
serve with the hot sauce.

Serves 4-6.

TURKEY CRANBERRY DIP

350g (12oz/1½ cups) sugar
450g (1lb) fresh cranberries
2 tablespoons port
1kg (2¼lb) cooked, diced turkey or chicken

In a large saucepan, put sugar and 425ml (15fl oz/scant 2 cups) water. Heat gently, stirring to dissolve sugar, then boil for 5 minutes.

Add cranberries and simmer for about 10 minutes until skins pop.

Remove from heat and stir in port. Pour mixture into fondue pot. Serve with diced turkey or chicken for dipping.

Serves 6.

HARISSA SPICED CHICKEN

2 teaspoons coriander seeds
1½ teaspoons cumin seeds
2 cloves garlic
1-2 tablespoons chilli paste
½ teaspoon salt
4 tablespoons olive oil
700g (1½lb) skinless, boneless chicken breasts
oil, for cooking
Couscous Salad (see page 91), to serve
TOMATO & PRESERVED LEMON SALSA:
3-4 ripe tomatoes
½ preserved lemon
2 spring onions, chopped
2 tablespoons liquid from the preserved lemons
1 tablespoon chopped fresh mint
salt and freshly ground black pepper

Heat a heavy based frying pan. Add coriander and cumin seeds, and dry fry, stirring, for 2 or 3 minutes until they give off a fragrant aroma. (See above.) Grind to a powder in a mortar and pestle. Place ground seeds in a bowl with garlic, chilli paste, salt and olive oil. Mix together. Cut chicken into cubes and add to marinade. Cover and leave in the fridge for 1 hour. Make the salsa. Cut tomatoes into dice and place in a bowl. Remove flesh from preserved lemon and cut rind into dice.

Add to tomatoes with spring onion, preserved lemon liquid, mint, salt and pepper. Transfer to small serving bowls. Remove chicken from marinade and dry with paper towels. Arrange on serving plates. Heat oil in the fondue pot on top of the stove then transfer to the lighted spirit burner. Spear chicken on to fondue forks and cook in hot oil for 3-4 minutes. Serve with the salsa and couscous.

Serves 4.

CHICKEN TIKKA

5cm (2in) piece fresh root ginger
4 tablespoons natural yogurt
1-2 tablespoons hot Madras curry paste
2 cloves garlic, crushed
1 teaspoon turmeric
2 tablespoons lemon juice
1 teaspoon paprika
½ teaspoon salt
700g (1½lb) skinless, boneless chicken breasts
coriander sprigs and lemon wedges, to garnish
oil, for cooking
TO SERVE:
Raita (see page 45)
naan bread
poppadoms

JERK CHICKEN

grated rind and juice 1 lime
2.5cm (1in) piece fresh root ginger
3 tablespoons olive oil
1 clove garlic, crushed
1 teaspoon dried thyme
1 teaspoon ground cinnamon
1 teaspoon ground allspice
1 teaspoon soft brown sugar
2 teaspoons hot pepper sauce
salt and freshly ground black pepper
900g (2lb) skinless, boneless chicken breasts
lime wedges, to garnish
oil, for frying
Bean Salad (see page 94), to serve

Peel ginger and grate into a bowl. Add the yogurt, curry paste, garlic, turmeric, lemon juice, paprika and salt. Mix together thoroughly. (See above.) Cut chicken into 2cm (¾in) cubes. Add to marinade and mix well. Cover and leave in the fridge to marinate for at least 2 hours. Remove from marinade and allow as much of the marinade to drain off as possible.

Grate rind from lime and squeeze juice into a bowl. Peel ginger and grate into the bowl. Add olive oil, garlic, thyme, cinnamon, allspice, sugar, hot pepper sauce, salt and pepper. Mix together. (See above.) Cut chicken into 2.5cm (1in) cubes and add to marinade. Cover and leave in a cool place to marinate for 2 hours.

Thread chicken cubes, 2 or 3 together, on to bamboo skewers and arrange on serving plates, garnished with coriander and lemon wedges. Heat oil in the fondue pot on top of the stove then transfer to the lighted spirit burner. Cook chicken in hot oil for 3-4 minutes until cooked. Serve with the raita, naan bread and poppadoms.

Serves 4.

Remove chicken from marinade, pat dry with paper towels and arrange on serving plates. Garnish with lime wedges. Heat oil in the fondue pot on top of the stove then transfer to the lighted spirit burner. Spear chicken on to fondue forks and cook in hot oil for 3-4 minutes until cooked. Serve with the salad.

Serves 6.

CHICKEN GOUJONS

THAI CHICKEN HOTPOT

700g (1½lb) skinless, boneless chicken breasts
seasoned flour, for dusting
3 eggs, beaten
85g (3oz/¾ cup) dry breadcrumbs
oil, for cooking
RED PEPPER SAUCE:
25g (1oz/6 teaspoons) butter
1 small onion, chopped
2 red peppers, seeded and chopped
1 clove garlic, crushed
225ml (8fl oz/1 cup) chicken stock
salt and freshly ground black pepper
sprig of dill, to garnish

Cut chicken in long strips about 1cm
(½in) wide.

Dust with seasoned flour, dip in egg, then
coat with breadcrumbs. Place in refrigerator
to chill. To make red pepper sauce, in a small
saucepan melt butter, add onion and cook
until soft. Add red peppers and garlic and
continue to cook over a gentle heat for
5 minutes. Pour in stock and simmer for
10 minutes or until peppers are tender.

900g (2lb) boneless chicken breasts
12 button mushrooms
12 spring onions, cut into 5cm (2in) lengths
1 red pepper, seeded and cut into strips
115g (4oz) baby sweetcorn
115g (4oz) mange-tout
1 bunch watercress
115g (4oz) fine egg noodles, broken into pieces
850ml (30fl oz/3¾ cups) good chicken stock
2 small red chillies
3 kaffir lime leaves
1 stalk lemon grass, crushed
2 slices fresh galangal or ginger
1 carrot, cut into thin matchsticks
6 Chinese leaves, shredded
Thai Dipping Sauce (see page 55), to serve

Cut chicken into thin strips, place on
6 serving plates, cover and chill until
required. Divide mushrooms, spring onions,
pepper, sweetcorn, mange-tout and
watercress between 6 plates, cover and chill
until required. Soak the egg noodles in
boiling water for 3-4 minutes, then drain and
transfer to a serving bowl. (See above.) Place
stock in a saucepan or fondue pot. Add
chillies, lime leaves, lemon grass and
galangal or ginger. Bring to the boil and
simmer gently for 10 minutes. Add carrot.

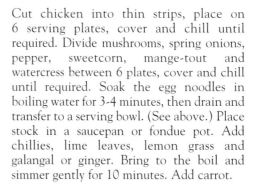

Sieve red pepper sauce, season with salt and
pepper and reheat. Heat oil in the fondue
pot on top of the stove then transfer to the
lighted spirit burner. Cook chicken goujons
in the hot oil. Garnish sauce with sprig of
dill and serve hot with the goujons.

Serves 6.

Either transfer stock to a hot pot or transfer
the fondue pot to the spirit burner. Using
chopsticks or Chinese wire strainers, cook
chicken and vegetables in the stock then dip
in the dipping sauce to eat. When this is
completed, add noodles and Chinese leaves
and ladle noodle soup into warmed bowls.

Serves 6-8.

THAI CHICKEN MEATBALLS

450g (1lb) minced chicken
4 spring onions, chopped
2 tablespoons chopped fresh coriander
2 tablespoons Thai green curry paste
1 teaspoon light muscovado sugar
1 teaspoon salt
lime wedges, to garnish
oil, for cooking
THAI DIPPING SAUCE:
1 fresh red chilli, seeded and finely chopped
2 tablespoons light soy sauce
1 tablespoon Thai fish sauce
1 tablespoon lime juice
2 tablespoons soft brown sugar

In a bowl, mix together chicken, spring onions, coriander, curry paste, sugar and salt. (See above.) Form into small balls. Cover and chill for 30 minutes. Make the dipping sauce. Place chilli, soy sauce, fish sauce, lime juice and sugar in a bowl and mix together. Divide between 4 small dip dishes.

Arrange chicken balls on serving plates and garnish with lime wedges. Heat oil in the fondue pot on top of the stove then transfer to the lighted spirit burner. Spear chicken balls on to fondue forks and cook in hot oil for 3-4 minutes. Serve with the dipping sauce.

Serves 4.

SAVOURY PARCELS

50g (2oz/¼ cup) butter
2 shallots, finely chopped
175g (6oz) lean bacon, chopped
450g (1lb) chicken livers, trimmed and chopped
225g (8oz) mushrooms, chopped
8 tablespoons chicken stock
2 egg yolks
pinch mixed dried herbs
salt and freshly ground black pepper
3-4 sheets filo pastry
1 egg white
oil, for cooking

Melt the butter in a large frying pan, add shallots and cook for 2 minutes.

Add bacon and cook for 3-4 minutes. Stir in chicken livers and cook for 3 minutes, then add mushrooms and cook for 3 minutes. Pour stock into pan and simmer until it has almost evaporated. Cool slightly, then stir in egg yolks, herbs and season with salt and pepper. Put mixture in a blender or food processor and chop coarsely. Leave to cool.

Cut pastry into 18-24 x 15cm (6in) squares. Place a tablespoon of chicken liver mixture at one end of each square. Fold over each side, then roll up parcel so it resembles a spring roll. Seal the edges with egg white, then set aside until needed. Heat oil in the fondue pot on top of the stove then transfer to the lighted spirit burner. Cook parcels in hot oil, using Chinese wire strainers for cooking and lifting them from hot oil.

Serves 6.

MONGOLIAN HOTPOT

1.35kg (3lb) lean lamb, leg or fillet
1.7 litres (60fl oz/7½ cups) chicken stock
1 teaspoon peeled, grated fresh root ginger
1 clove garlic, crushed
2 tablespoons chopped spring onion
2 tablespoons chopped fresh coriander
115g (4oz) spinach leaves, shredded
225g (8oz) Chinese leaves, shredded
85g (3oz) instant soup noodles
HOTPOT DIPPING SAUCE:
6 tablespoons soy sauce
3 tablespoons smooth peanut butter
2 tablespoons rice wine or dry sherry
pinch chilli powder
3 tablespoons hot water

Slice lamb very thinly and arrange on two large plates. Put stock into a large saucepan with ginger and garlic and simmer for 15 minutes. Put spring onion, coriander, spinach, Chinese leaves and noodles into separate serving bowls. Combine the ingredients for dipping sauce and divide between 6 small dishes.

Put stock into a special Mongolian hotpot or a fondue pot. Add spring onions and bring back to the boil. Transfer pot to burner. Each person uses a fondue fork, or Chinese wire strainer, to cook pieces of food in stock. The food is then dipped in sauce before eating. Any remaining spinach and Chinese leaves are finally added to the pot with coriander and noodles. When noodles are tender the soup is served in bowls.

Serves 6.

CANTONESE HOTPOT

225g (8oz) rump steak, fat removed
350g (12oz) skinless, boneless chicken breasts
115g (4oz) mange-tout
225g (8oz) peeled prawns
1 red pepper, seeded and cut into strips
115g (4oz) button mushrooms, halved
225g (8oz) can bamboo shoots, drained
1.7 litres (60fl oz/7½ cups) chicken stock
2 teaspoons peeled, chopped fresh root ginger
50g (2oz) fine egg noodles
YELLOW BEAN SAUCE:
1 tablespoon soy sauce
2 tablespoons yellow bean sauce
1 tablespoon dry sherry
1 fresh green chilli, seeded and finely chopped

Slice steak and chicken thinly and arrange on 6 individual plates. Top and tail mange-tout and arrange on plates with prawns and remaining vegetables. Put stock into a large saucepan with ginger and simmer for 15 minutes. Soak egg noodles in warm water for 10 minutes, then drain and put into a serving bowl. In a bowl, combine ingredients for yellow bean sauce, then add 2 tablespoons water and divide between 6 small dishes.

Pour stock into fondue pot, bring back to simmering; place over burner. Each person uses a fondue fork, or Chinese wire strainer, to cook pieces of food in stock. The cooked food is then dipped in sauce before eating. When all the meat and vegetables have been eaten, add noodles to fondue pot to heat through, then ladle soup into bowls.

Serves 6.

VEGETABLES

CAULIFLOWER CHEESE

1 cauliflower
crisp fried onions, to garnish
CHEESE SAUCE:
15g (½oz/1 tablespoon) butter
2 shallots, finely chopped
15g (½oz/2 tablespoons) plain flour
300ml (10fl oz/1½ cups) milk
50g (2oz/½ cup) grated Cheddar cheese
25g (1oz/¼ cup) grated Parmesan cheese
1 teaspoon Dijon mustard
pinch cayenne pepper
salt

Cut cauliflower into florets. Bring a pan of salted water to the boil.

Add cauliflower and boil for 5 minutes or until just tender. Drain thoroughly and divide between 4 serving plates. To make the cheese sauce, place butter in a saucepan and heat gently until melted. Add shallots and cook for 5 minutes until soft. Stir in flour and cook for 1 minute. Remove the pan from the heat and gradually stir in milk. Return the pan to the heat and bring to the boil then simmer gently, stirring for 2 minutes.

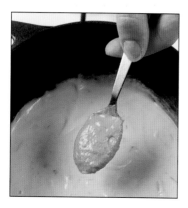

Stir in Cheddar cheese, Parmesan cheese, mustard and cayenne pepper. Season with salt. Transfer the fondue pot to the lighted spirit burner. Scatter fried onions over the top. Spear the cauliflower florets on to fondue forks and dip into the sauce.

Serves 4.

FALAFEL FONDUE

225g (8oz/1 cup) dried chickpeas, soaked overnight
  in cold water and drained
2 tablespoons chopped fresh parsley
1 tablespoon chopped fresh coriander
1 tablespoon tahini paste
1 clove garlic, crushed
1 tablespoon lemon juice
salt and freshly ground black pepper
seasoned flour, for dusting
oil, for frying
warm pitta bread, to serve
CHILLI YOGURT DIP:
150ml (5fl oz/⅔ cup) Greek yogurt
1 fresh red chilli, seeded and finely chopped
2 tablespoons chopped fresh coriander

Process chickpeas in a blender or food processor until as smooth as possible. Transfer to a bowl and stir in parsley, coriander, tahini, garlic, lemon juice and salt and pepper. (See above.) Cover and set aside for 30 minutes. To make the chilli dip, in a bowl, mix together the yogurt, chilli, coriander, salt and pepper. Transfer to a serving bowl and set aside.

With floured hands, roll the chickpea mixture into 2.5cm (1in) balls. Dust with seasoned flour. Arrange on serving plates. Heat oil in the fondue pot on top of the stove then transfer to the lighted spirit burner. Spear the falafel on to fondue forks and cook in the hot oil for 2 minutes or until evenly browned. Serve with the chilli yogurt dip and warm pitta bread.

Serves 4.

CAULIFLOWER FRITTERS

1 cauliflower, cut into florets
85g (3oz/¾ cup) dried breadcrumbs
40g (1½oz/⅓ cup) grated Parmesan cheese
1 tablespoon chopped fresh parsley
salt and freshly ground black pepper
2-3 eggs, beaten
oil, for cooking
CHEDDAR CHEESE SAUCE:
15g (½oz/3 teaspoons) butter
15g (½oz/6 teaspoons) plain flour
300ml (10fl oz/11¼ cups) milk
1/2 teaspoon prepared mustard
50g (2oz/½ cup) grated Cheddar cheese
pinch cayenne pepper

Parboil cauliflower in a saucepan of boiling salted water for 4-5 minutes; drain well. (See above.) In a bowl, mix together breadcrumbs, Parmesan cheese and parsley and season with salt and pepper. Dip cauliflower florets in beaten egg, then coat in breadcrumb mixture. Put on to a serving plate and set aside until ready to cook.

To make cheese sauce, melt butter in a small saucepan, stir in flour and cook for 1 minute. Remove from heat and add milk slowly. Bring to the boil, stirring, then simmer for 2 minutes. Stir in mustard, cheese, cayenne and season with salt and pepper. Keep hot. Heat oil in the fondue pot on top of the stove then transfer to the lighted spirit burner. Cook the cauliflower in the oil and serve with the hot sauce.

Serves 4-6.

SPRING ROLLS

1 tablespoon oil
1 teaspoon sesame oil
1 clove garlic, crushed
1 fresh red chilli, seeded and finely sliced
450g (1lb) pack fresh stir-fry vegetables
2cm (½in) piece fresh root ginger, grated
1 tablespoon dry sherry or rice wine
1 tablespoon soy sauce
salt and freshly ground black pepper
12 spring roll wrappers
1 small egg, beaten
lime wedges and fresh coriander, to garnish
oil, for frying
Ginger Dipping Sauce (see page 64), to serve

Heat oils in a wok. Add garlic and chilli.

Stir-fry for 30 seconds. Add vegetables and ginger and stir-fry for 1 minute more, then drizzle sherry or rice wine and soy sauce over. Allow mixture to bubble up for 1 minute. Season with salt and pepper. Using a slotted spoon, transfer the vegetables to a dish. Set aside until cool. Soften the spring roll wrappers, following the directions on the packet. Place a spoonful of filling on a wrapper.

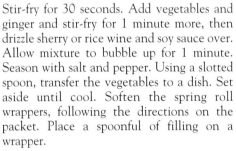

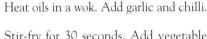

Fold over front edge and sides and roll up neatly, sealing edges with a little beaten egg. Repeat with remaining wrappers and filling. Divide spring rolls between 4 serving plates. Garnish with lime wedges and coriander. Heat oil in the fondue pot on top of the stove then transfer to the lighted spirit burner. Dip rolls into oil, using fondue forks or Chinese wire baskets. Cook for 2 minutes or until crisp. Serve with the dipping sauce.

Serves 4.

ONION BHAJI FONDUE

4 tablespoons gram flour
½ teaspoon turmeric
½ teaspoon ground cumin
½ teaspoon ground coriander
1 teaspoon garam masala
pinch cayenne pepper
1 egg, beaten
1 large onion, quartered and very thinly sliced
1 tablespoon chopped fresh coriander
oil, for frying
MINTED YOGURT DIP:
225ml (8fl oz/1 cup) Greek yogurt
1 clove garlic, crushed
3 tablespoons chopped fresh mint
salt and freshly ground black pepper

To make the dip, in a bowl mix together yogurt, garlic, mint, salt and pepper. (See above.) Transfer to serving bowls and set aside. Put the gram flour, turmeric, cumin, coriander, garam masala and cayenne pepper in a bowl and mix together. Stir in egg, season with salt and pepper then add sliced onion and chopped coriander. Heat the oil in the fondue pot on top of the stove then transfer to the lighted spirit burner.

To cook the bhajis, push teaspoons of mixture into oil with another spoon. Cook a few at a time for 2-3 minutes until crisp and golden. Remove from oil with Chinese wire nets. Serve with the yogurt dip.

Serves 4 as an appetiser.

SWISS POTATOES

1kg (2lb) small new potatoes, scrubbed
2 eggs, beaten
115g (4oz/1 cup) herb stuffing mix
oil, for cooking
GARLIC SAUCE:
115g (4oz/2 cups) fresh white breadcrumbs
2 cloves garlic
salt and freshly ground black pepper
225ml (8fl oz/1 cup) olive oil
4 teaspoons lemon juice
1 tablespoon white wine vinegar

Boil potatoes in skins until just tender; drain and cool. Dip in beaten egg, then roll in stuffing mix and set aside.

To make garlic sauce, dampen breadcrumbs with 1 tablespoon water. Put into a blender or food processor with garlic and ½ teaspoon salt and blend together until well mixed. Add oil a little at a time and continue to process until all the oil has been added.

Work the lemon juice and vinegar into the sauce until if forms a smooth, creamy consistency. Season with pepper. Turn mixture into a bowl. Heat the oil in the fondue pot on top of the stove then transfer to the lighted spirit burner. Spear the potatoes and cook in the hot oil; serve with the sauce.

Serves 4-6.

Note: Serve the potatoes also with Cheddar Cheese Sauce (see page 59).

SPICY CHICKPEA BALLS

115g (4oz/¾ cup) bulgar wheat
115ml (4fl oz/½ cup) boiling water
225g (8oz/1¼ cups) chickpeas, soaked overnight
2 tablespoons sunflower oil
2 cloves garlic, crushed
½ teaspoon baking powder
1 teaspoon chilli powder
1 teaspoon each ground coriander and ground cumin
salt and freshly ground black pepper
oil, for cooking
FRESH TOMATO SAUCE:
4 tomatoes, peeled
½ green pepper, halved and seeded
½ red pepper, halved and seeded
1 fresh green chilli, cored and seeded
1 tablespoon fresh coriander, chopped

Put the bulgar wheat into a bowl, pour the boiling water over and leave the wheat to soak for 1 hour. Drain chickpeas and put into a food processor with bulgar wheat and remaining ingredients (except cooking oil and those for sauce). Blend for a few minutes until mixture becomes fairly smooth. With your hands, mould the mixture into 36 small balls and place on a serving dish.

To make the fresh tomato sauce, put all the ingredients into a blender or food processor and process until vegetables are finely chopped. Add seasoning, then put into a serving bowl. Heat the oil in the fondue pot on top of the stove then transfer to the lighted spirit burner. Spear the chickpea balls and cook in the hot oil. Serve with the fresh tomato sauce.

Serves 4-6.

ASPARAGUS FONDUE

425g (15oz) canned asparagus spears
1 clove garlic, halved
225ml (8fl oz/1 cup) dry white wine
350g (12oz) Edam cheese, grated
1 tablespoon cornflour
4 tablespoons crème fraîche
salt and freshly ground black pepper
TO SERVE:
blanched fresh asparagus spears, cooked baby
  artichoke hearts, cubes of French bread

Drain asparagus and process in a blender or food processor until smooth. Set aside.

Rub the inside of the fondue pot with garlic, then pour in wine and heat until bubbling. Gradually stir in cheese and cook, stirring, over a low heat, until cheese has melted. Blend together cornflour and crème fraîche and stir into cheese mixture. Continue to cook for a few more minutes until thick and smooth.

Stir in asparagus purée and season with salt and pepper. Cook for another minute until heated through. Transfer the pot to the lighted burner. Serve with the asparagus spears, artichoke hearts and bread.

Serves 4-6.

PUMPKIN FONDUE

4 small pumpkins or squash, the size of a grapefruit
300g (10oz) creamy blue cheese such as dolcelatte
225ml (8fl oz/1 cup) double cream
4 tablespoons fresh white breadcrumbs
2 teaspoons chopped fresh sage
salt and freshly ground black pepper
HERB BREADSTICKS:
450g (1lb) packet ciabatta bread mix
1 tablespoon dried oregano
1 tablespoon caraway seeds
oil, for brushing
flour, for dusting

Preheat the oven to 230C (450F/Gas 8). To make breadsticks, follow packet instructions to after first rising of dough.

Turn dough on to a floured board, add oregano and caraway seeds and knead again. Roll out to approximately 5mm (¼in) thickness and slice into 2cm (¾in) lengths. Brush a baking sheet with oil. Arrange breadsticks on baking sheet and leave in a warm place for about 10 minutes to rise. Dust with flour and bake for 15 minutes or until browned. Leave to cool and set aside. Reduce the oven temperature to 190C (375F/Gas 5). Slice the tops off pumpkins and scoop out the seeds and fibres.

Crumble half the cheese into pumpkins; top with half the cream. Scatter 1 tablespoon of breadcrumbs in each pumpkin then top with remaining cheese and cream. Scatter sage over and season with salt and pepper. Replace tops on pumpkins then place in an ovenproof dish. Bake for 45 minutes or until cheese is bubbling and pumpkins are soft. Serve with breadsticks to dip in then scrape out pumpkin flesh with a spoon.

Serves 4.

MIXED VEGETABLE KEBABS

4 courgettes, cut into slices
16 button mushrooms
1 red pepper, seeded and cut into chunks
1 green pepper, seeded and cut into chunks
oil, for cooking
CREAMY ONION SAUCE:
115g (4oz/½ cup) low fat soft cheese
150ml (5fl oz/⅔ cup) natural yogurt
½ bunch spring onions, finely chopped
BATTER:
2 large eggs
125g (4oz/1 cup) plain flour

Thread the vegetables on to 12-16 bamboo skewers.

To make the creamy onion sauce, mix all the ingredients together and put into a serving bowl.

Make batter. Put eggs into a bowl with 200ml (7fl oz/scant 1 cup) iced water and beat until frothy. Add flour and beat until just blended – do not worry if a few lumps are left. Pour into a bowl or jug and stand it in a bowl of ice. Heat the oil in the fondue pot on top of the stove then transfer to the lighted spirit burner. To cook kebabs, each person dips a skewer into the batter, then into hot oil to cook until the batter is golden. The kebabs are then eaten with the onion sauce.

Serves 4.

AUBERGINE FRITTERS

450g (1lb) aubergines, diced
1-2 teaspoons salt
seasoned flour, for dusting
oil, for cooking
BATTER:
115g (4oz/1 cup) plain flour
2 eggs, separated
2 tablespoons olive oil
COOL CURRY DIP:
2 teaspoons curry paste
1 teaspoon Dijon mustard
2 teaspoons brown sugar
4 teaspoons grated onion
6 tablespoons mayonnaise
6 tablespoons natural yogurt

Put aubergine in a colander, add salt. (See above.) Leave aubergine to stand for 30 minutes. To make batter, sift flour and ¼ teaspoon salt into a bowl, beat in egg yolks and oil. Gradually add 175ml (6fl oz/¾ cup) water and continue to beat to make a smooth batter. Leave to stand for 1 hour. Just before serving, whisk egg whites until stiff and fold into batter.

To make cool curry dip, whisk all ingredients together in a bowl, then spoon into a serving dish. Rinse aubergine under cold, running water and dry thoroughly on paper towels. Dust diced aubergine with seasoned flour. Heat the oil in the fondue pot on top of the stove then transfer to the lighted spirit burner. To cook fritters, each piece of aubergine is dipped into batter, then cooked in hot oil in the fondue pot.

Serves 4.

CHEESE & TOMATO FONDUE

500g (1lb) carton passata
200g (7oz/scant 1 cup) cream cheese
sugar, to taste
few drops Tabasco sauce
salt and freshly ground black pepper
frankfurters and cubes of ham, to serve
CORNMEAL MUFFINS:
50g (2oz/½ cup) self-raising flour
1½ teaspoons baking powder
salt and freshly ground black pepper
115g (4oz/1 cup) fine cornmeal
50g (2oz/½ cup) grated Cheddar cheese
25g (1oz/2 tablespoons) butter, melted
1 large egg, beaten
150ml (5fl oz/⅔ cup) milk

Preheat the oven to 200C (400F/Gas 6). Line 12 mini muffin pans with paper mini muffin cases. To make the muffins, sift flour, baking powder, salt and pepper into a bowl then stir in cornmeal and cheese. (See above.) In a bowl, mix together butter, egg and milk. Pour on to the dry ingredients and mix quickly until just combined. Do not overmix. Spoon the batter into prepared muffin cases. Bake for 10-15 minutes until well risen and golden brown. Leave to cool. Arrange on serving plates with the frankfurters and ham.

Place passata and cream cheese in a fondue pot and heat gently until cheese has melted. Add sugar, Tabasco sauce, salt and pepper to taste. Heat until just below simmering point then transfer to the fondue burner. Serve with the corn muffins, frankfurters and ham for dipping.

Serves 4-6.

TEMPURA

oil, for frying
450g (1lb) assorted vegetables, such as red pepper strips, aubergine and courgette batons, spring onions, mushrooms, mange-tout, baby sweetcorn, asparagus
BATTER:
115g (4oz/1 cup) plain flour
1 egg, separated
1 teaspoon olive oil
salt and freshly ground black pepper
GINGER DIPPING SAUCE:
2 teaspoons each sesame oil, red wine vinegar and soy sauce
3 tablespoons ginger syrup (from jar of ginger)
2 tablespoons clear honey
4 spring onions, finely sliced

To make the batter, sift flour into a bowl. Measure 225ml (8fl oz/1 cup) iced water into a jug and whisk in egg yolk and olive oil. Season with salt and pepper. Make a well in the middle of flour and gradually whisk in liquid. (See above.) Cover and stand for 1 hour. To make the dipping sauce, mix together the sesame oil, red wine vinegar, soy sauce, ginger syrup and honey. Transfer to small dishes and sprinkle the spring onions on top.

Whisk egg white until stiff then fold into the batter. Heat oil in the fondue pot on top of the stove then transfer to the lighted spirit burner. To serve, dip vegetables into batter then into hot oil for 1-2 minutes until crisp and browned. Alternatively, spear two or three pieces of vegetables on to skewers and cook in the hot oil. Serve with the dipping sauce.

Serves 4.

AVOCADO FONDUE

2 avocados
1 tablespoon lime juice
1 clove garlic
225ml (8fl oz/1 cup) dry white wine
350g (12oz) Gruyère cheese, grated
1 tablespoon cornflour
salt and freshly ground black pepper
4 tablespoons sour cream
TO SERVE:
pickled jalapeño chillies, slices of apple, breadsticks, large peeled prawns

Halve avocados and remove stones. Using a teaspoon, scoop out flesh and place in a bowl. Scrape out all bright green flesh next to skin.

Mash avocado until smooth then stir in lime juice. Cut garlic in half and rub round inside of the fondue pot. Pour in wine and heat until bubbling. In a bowl, toss together cheese and cornflour then stir into the wine. Cook gently, stirring, until cheese has melted.

Add avocado and cook, stirring, until smooth and heated through. Season with salt and pepper then stir in sour cream. Transfer the pot to the lighted burner and serve with the chillies, apple, breadsticks and prawns for dipping.

Serves 4-6.

WILD MUSHROOM FONDUE

7g (¼oz) dried wild mushrooms
3 tablespoons olive oil
4 shallots, finely chopped
2 cloves garlic, crushed
115g (4oz) fresh mixed wild mushrooms, chopped
3 tablespoons plain flour
225ml (8fl oz/1 cup) dry cider
350g (12oz) Emmental cheese, grated
115g (4oz) Roquefort cheese, crumbled
1 tablespoon chopped fresh tarragon
2 tablespoons single cream
TO SERVE:
cubes of ham, cherry tomatoes, cooked asparagus
  spears and cubes of bread

Place dried mushrooms in a bowl and cover with boiling water. Leave to soak for 20 minutes. Drain, reserving 115ml (4fl oz/ ½ cup) of soaking liquid. Chop soaked mushrooms finely. (See above.) In the fondue pot, heat the oil. Add shallots and garlic and cook for 5 minutes until soft. Add dried and fresh mushrooms and cook for a further 4-5 minutes until soft. Stir in flour and cook for 2 minutes. Gradually stir in reserved soaking liquid, then add cider.

Cook gently, stirring, until the mixture thickens then gradually stir in Emmental and Roquefort cheeses. Add the tarragon and continue to cook gently, stirring until the cheese is melted and the mixture is smooth and creamy. Stir in cream. Transfer pot to the lighted burner and serve with the ham, vegetables and bread to dip in.

Serves 6.

BLACK-EYED BEAN DIP

225g (8oz/1 cup) black-eyed beans, soaked overnight
  in cold water
1 clove garlic
few sprigs parsley
½ teaspoon salt
50g (2oz/1¼ cup) butter
1 onion, chopped
1 teaspoon curry paste
150ml (5fl oz/⅔ cup) natural yogurt
CURRIED BREAD CUBES:
1 small white loaf
vegetable oil, for frying
3 teaspoons curry powder

Drain soaking water from beans.

Add enough fresh water to cover beans, add garlic and parsley and simmer for about 1 hour until beans are tender. Stir salt into beans and cook for a further 5 minutes; drain and discard parsley. In a small saucepan, melt butter, add onion and cook until tender. Put beans and onion into a blender or food processor and blend until puréed. Put bean purée into a fondue pot, stir in curry paste and yogurt and reheat.

To make curried bread cubes, cut crusts off loaf, then cut bread into cubes. Heat oil in a frying pan and fry bread until crisp and golden, then drain on paper towels. Sprinkle with curry powder and toss together. To eat, spear bread cubes with fondue forks and dip into bean fondue.

Serves 4-6.

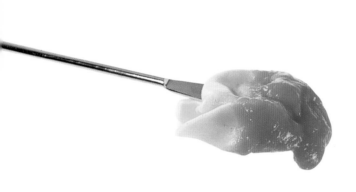

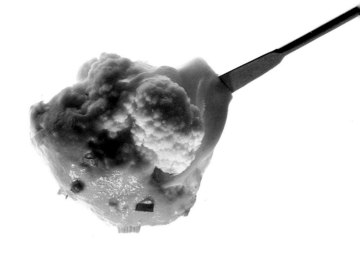

PEPPER & TOMATO FONDUE

6 large tomatoes
4 red peppers
5 tablespoons olive oil
1 clove garlic, chopped
salt and freshly ground black pepper
1 onion, finely chopped
150ml (5fl oz/⅔ cup) vegetable or chicken stock
2 tablespoons cornflour, blended with a little water
fresh ravioli, cooked, to serve

Preheat the oven to 190C (375F/Gas 5). Oil 2 roasting tins. Cut tomatoes in half and cut red peppers into quarters and remove the seeds.

Place tomatoes, cut side up, in one of the roasting tins. Drizzle with 2 tablespoons of the olive oil and scatter with garlic. Season with salt and pepper. Place peppers in the other tin and drizzle with 2 tablespoons olive oil. Put tomatoes and peppers in the oven and roast tomatoes for 45-60 minutes until beginning to blacken round the edges. Cook the peppers, turning occasionally, until their skins are charred and blistered. Put in a plastic bag, seal and leave until cool enough to handle, then peel and chop coarsely.

Heat remaining oil in a pan. Cook onion, stirring occasionally, for 5-10 minutes, until soft. Add peppers and stock. Cover and simmer for 15 minutes. Transfer to a blender or food processor, add tomatoes and process until smooth. Press through a sieve and pour into the fondue pot. Heat on the stove until almost simmering. Stir cornflour into mixture. Simmer for a few minutes until thickened then transfer to the lighted fondue burner. Serve with the ravioli.

Serves 4.

LEEK PURÉE

1kg (2lb) leeks, coarsely chopped
150ml (5fl oz/⅔ cup) chicken stock
50g (2oz/¼ cup) butter
salt and freshly ground black pepper
pinch freshly grated nutmeg
2 spring onions, finely chopped
raw cauliflower florets, carrot sticks and button mushrooms, to serve

Wash the leeks well, then put into a saucepan with 1 tablespoon water and cook for 10-15 minutes until soft.

Drain leeks and leave to cool slightly. Purée leeks in a blender of food processor with stock until smooth.

Spoon purée into fondue pot. Place over a gentle heat and beat in butter and season with salt, pepper and nutmeg. Stir in spring onions and keep warm on a lighted spirit burner. Serve with a selection of raw vegetables or as an accompaniment to grilled meat.

Serves 4-6.

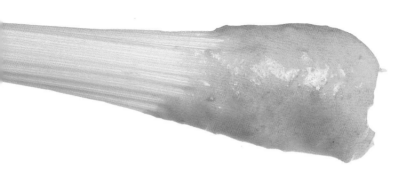

TOMATO NIÇOISE

50g (2oz/¼ cup) butter
700g (1½lb) ripe tomatoes
1 clove garlic, crushed
1 small onion, chopped
175g (6oz) can pimentoes, drained and chopped
salt and freshly ground black pepper
pinch sugar
2 tablespoons mayonnaise
cooked artichoke leaves, cooked green beans, strips
  of cucumber and celery, to serve

Melt butter in a saucepan, add tomatoes, garlic, onion and pimento and cook gently for 10-15 minutes until soft.

Sieve mixture into a bowl; season with salt, pepper and sugar and leave to cool. Whisk in mayonnaise.

Pour the tomato Niçoise into a serving bowl. To serve, arrange the vegetables on a large platter and stand the bowl in the centre.

Serves 4-6.

MUSHROOM FONDUE

50g (2oz/¼ cup) butter
450g (1lb) mushrooms, finely chopped
2 cloves garlic, crushed
150ml (5fl oz/⅔ cup) chicken stock
150ml (5fl oz/⅔ cup) double cream
3 teaspoons cornflour
salt and freshly ground black pepper
pinch cayenne pepper
cubes of cheese and garlic sausage, to serve

Melt butter in a saucepan, add mushrooms and garlic and cook gently for 10 minutes.

Add stock and simmer for 10 minutes. Cool slightly and purée in a blender or food processor.

Put a little cream into the fondue pot, blend in cornflour smoothly, then add remaining cream and the mushroom purée. Heat to a simmer and cook over a gentle heat until thickened, stirring frequently. Season with salt, pepper and cayenne. Serve with cubes of cheese and garlic sausage.

Serves 4-6.

SWEETCORN FONDUE

450g (1lb) frozen sweetcorn kernels
2 teaspoons cornflour
3 tablespoons single cream
salt and freshly ground black pepper
few drops Tabasco sauce
25g (1oz/6 teaspoons) butter
selection of cooked prawns and mussels, to serve

Put sweetcorn into a saucepan with 2 tablespoons water and simmer for a few minutes until tender.

Drain the corn and put into a blender or food processor and process until soft but not too smooth. In a saucepan, blend cornflour smoothly with cream. Add sweetcorn mixture and cook over a low heat until smooth.

Pour mixture into fondue pot, season with salt, pepper and Tabasco sauce, then beat in butter. Set pot over a low burner to keep warm. Serve with selection of cooked shellfish.

Serves 4-6.

THAI SWEETCORN FONDUE

400g (14oz) canned sweetcorn
300ml (10fl oz/1¼ cups) chicken stock
200ml (7fl oz/scant 1 cup) coconut cream
1 tablespoon Thai green curry paste
1 tablespoon Thai fish sauce
2 tablespoons cornflour
2 tablespoons chopped fresh coriander
TO SERVE:
blanched baby sweetcorn and mange-tout
mini poppadoms
cooked peeled prawns

Drain sweetcorn. In a blender or food processor, process sweetcorn to a purée and transfer to the fondue pot.

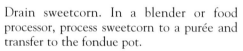
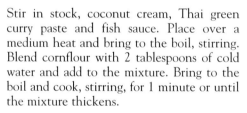

Stir in stock, coconut cream, Thai green curry paste and fish sauce. Place over a medium heat and bring to the boil, stirring. Blend cornflour with 2 tablespoons of cold water and add to the mixture. Bring to the boil and cook, stirring, for 1 minute or until the mixture thickens.

Stir in the chopped coriander. Transfer the pot to the lighted fondue burner and serve with the baby sweetcorn, mange-tout, poppadoms and prawns.

Serves 4.

Note: Vary the amount of Thai green curry sauce according to taste. For children, add a little less and for those who prefer a more fiery flavour, add more.

DESSERTS

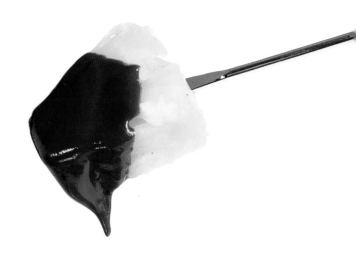

CLASSIC CHOCOLATE FONDUE

250g (9oz) plain chocolate
150ml (5fl oz/⅔ cup) double cream
2 tablespoons brandy
selection of fruit such as strawberries, pineapple,
  banana, physallis, figs and kiwi fruit, to serve
SPONGE FINGERS:
40g (1½oz) caster sugar
1 egg
25g (1oz/½ cup) plain flour, sifted

Preheat the oven to 190C (375C/Gas 5.)
Line a baking sheet with non-stick
parchment. To make sponge fingers, place
caster sugar and egg in a large bowl.

Set bowl over a pan of barely simmering
water and whisk together until thick and
mousse-like. (See above.) Remove bowl
from heat and gently fold in flour. Using a
piping bag fitted with a 1cm (½in) plain
nozzle, pipe finger lengths of mixture on to
the prepared baking sheet. Bake for 6-8
minutes until golden. Transfer sponge
fingers to a wire rack to cool.

Break up chocolate and place in the fondue
pot with cream and brandy. Heat gently,
stirring, until chocolate has melted and
mixture is smooth. Transfer fondue pot to
the lighted spirit burner and serve with the
sponge fingers and fruit.

Serves 4-6.

VARIATION: For children, substitute orange
juice for brandy.

CARIBBEAN CHOCOLATE FONDUE

1 pineapple
1 mango
2 bananas
juice ½ lime
350g (13oz) good quality plain chocolate
200ml (7fl oz/scant 1 cup) coconut cream
2 tablespoons white rum
½ teaspoon freshly grated nutmeg

Cut the leafy top and the bottom off
pineapple. Cut away skin and cut pineapple
into quarters, lengthways. Cut out core and
cut each quarter into cubes.

Peel mango then cut down on either side of
stone to remove flesh. Cut into cubes. Cut
bananas into slices and sprinkle with lime
juice.

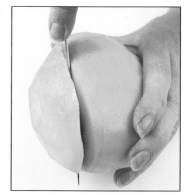

Break up chocolate into a fondue pot. Add
coconut cream and heat gently on the stove,
stirring, until chocolate melts. Stir in rum
and nutmeg, then place over a lighted spirit
burner to keep warm. Serve with the fruit.

Serves 6.

CHOCOLATE & HONEY FONDUE

300g (10oz) plain chocolate
1 heaped tablespoon honey
300ml (10fl oz/1¼ cups) double cream
SPICED FRUIT:
400g (14oz) ready-to-eat dried fruit such as apricots
  and prunes
1 cinnamon stick
1 star anise
4 cloves
1 tablespoon honey

To prepare the fruit, place in a saucepan and cover with water. Add cinnamon stick, star anise and cloves, and bring to the boil.

Stir in honey and remove from the heat. Set aside and leave until cold. Drain fruit and pat dry on paper towels. Arrange on 6 individual plates.

Break up the chocolate and place in the fondue pot with honey and cream. Heat gently, stirring, until chocolate has melted and mixture is smooth. Transfer the fondue pot to the lighted spirit burner and serve with the fruit.

Serves 6.

Note: For both the fondue and fruit, choose a fragrant blossom honey such as Mexican wildflower honey.

MOCHA TIA MARIA FONDUE

225g (8oz) plain chocolate
3 teaspoons instant coffee powder
155ml (5fl oz/⅔ cup) double cream
3 tablespoons Tia Maria
selection of fresh fruit, to serve
NUTTY MERINGUE:
2 egg whites
115g (4oz/½ cup) caster sugar
50g (2oz) flaked almonds, lightly toasted

To make meringues, preheat oven to 110C (225F/Gas ¼). Line 2 or 3 baking sheets with non-stick paper. Whisk egg whites until stiff, then fold in half the sugar and whisk again until stiff. Lightly fold in remaining sugar.

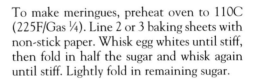

Put teaspoonfuls of mixture on to lined baking sheets to make a total of 30. Insert a few almonds into each one, then bake for 1½-2 hours until dry and crisp. Turn off oven, but leave meringues in oven to cool. Peel meringues off paper once they are cool.

To make mocha fondue, break up chocolate into a fondue pot, add coffee and cream and heat gently until melted, stirring all the time. Stir in Tia Maria and beat until smooth. Leave pot over a lighted spirit burner to keep warm. Serve with nutty meringues and fruit.

Serves 6.

CHOCOLATE NUT FONDUE

350g (12oz) Swiss chocolate with nuts
225ml (8fl oz/1 cup) double cream
2 tablespoons brandy or rum
selection of fresh fruit, to serve
VIENNESE FINGERS:
115g (4oz/½ cup) butter
25g (1oz/2 tablespoons) icing sugar
115g (4oz/1 cup) plain flour
¼ teaspoon baking powder
few drops vanilla essence

To make Viennese fingers, preheat oven to 190C (375F/Gas 5). Grease 2 or 3 baking sheets. Beat butter and icing sugar together in a bowl until pale and creamy.

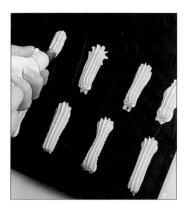

Add sifted flour, baking powder and vanilla essence and beat well. Put mixture into a piping bag fitted with 0.5cm (¼in) star nozzle and pipe 5cm (2in) fingers on to greased baking sheets, to make a total of 24. Bake in the oven for 15 minutes. Leave to cool on a wire rack.

To make chocolate fondue, break up chocolate into a fondue pot. Add cream and heat gently, stirring all the time until chocolate melts. Stir in brandy or rum, then leave over a lighted spirit burner to keep warm. Serve with Viennese fingers and fruit.

Serves 6.

BANANA & CHOCOLATE BITES

6 firm ripe bananas
115g (4oz/¾ cup) shelled pistachio nuts
225g (8oz) plain chocolate
4 tablespoons single cream

Peel bananas and cut them into 2.5cm (1in) lengths. Cover a metal baking sheet with clear film.

Arrange banana slices in a single layer on the baking sheet and place in the freezer. Leave in the freezer for at least 3 hours or until completely frozen. Coarsely chop pistachio nuts and divide between 4 small shallow dishes. When ready to serve, break up chocolate into the fondue pot. Add cream and heat gently on top of the stove, stirring, until chocolate is melted and mixture is smooth.

Transfer fondue pot to the lighted spirit burner. Bring banana pieces to the table on the metal baking sheet. To serve, spear the banana on to bamboo skewers or fondue forks, dip into the chocolate and then into the chopped nuts.

Serves 6.

CHOCOLATE ORANGE FONDUE

350g (12oz) plain chocolate chips
4 tablespoons double cream
50ml (2fl oz/¼ cup) orange juice
1 teaspoon grated orange rind
PROFITEROLES:
50g (2oz/¼ cup) butter
70g (2½oz) plain flour, sifted
2 eggs, lightly beaten
150ml (5fl oz/⅔ cup) double cream, whipped

Preheat the oven to 220C (425F/Gas 7). Butter 2 baking sheets. Make the profiteroles, place butter in a pan with 150ml (5fl oz/⅔ cup) water. Bring just to the boil and remove from the heat.

Add flour to pan, stirring constantly with a wooden spoon, until combined. (See above.) Return pan to heat and continue beating over a low heat until mixture is smooth and pulls away from sides of the pan. Remove from heat and leave to cool for a minute. Beat in eggs, a little at a time, until mixture is smooth and glossy. Using 2 spoons, place 24 walnut-sized mounds of mixture well apart on the baking sheets. Bake for 20 minutes until well risen and golden brown. Reduce oven temperature to 180C (350F/Gas 4). Make a hole in each bun.

Return buns to the oven for 5 minutes. Cool on a wire rack. Spoon a little cream into each bun. Place chocolate chips, cream and orange juice in a large microwave safe bowl. Cover and microwave at full power for 1 minute. Stir until smooth. Heat for a few more seconds, if necessary, until all the chocolate is melted. Stir in orange rind. Transfer to a fondue pot and place on a lighted burner. Spear profiteroles on to bamboo skewers or fondue forks, to serve.

Serves 4-6.

BLACK FOREST FONDUE

400g (14oz) can stoned black cherries
150ml (5fl oz/⅔ cup) double cream
1 tablespoon kirsch
1 tablespoon cornflour
CHOCOLATE CAKE:
2 eggs
115g (4oz/½ cup) softened butter
115g (4oz/½ cup) caster sugar
115g (4oz/1 cup) self-raising flour
½ teaspoon baking powder
2 tablespoons cocoa
1 tablespoon milk

Preheat the oven to 190C (375F/Gas 5). Grease a 17.5cm (7in) shallow, square tin.

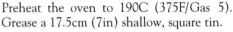

To make the chocolate cake, put eggs, butter and sugar into a bowl. (See above.) Sift flour, baking powder and cocoa over. Add milk and beat together until smooth. Turn mixture into prepared tin and bake for 25 minutes until cooked and firm to the touch. Turn on to a wire rack and leave to cool. Cut into small squares when cold.

Empty cherries and their juice into a blender or food processor and process until reasonably smooth. Transfer to a fondue pot, stir in cream and heat until simmering. Add kirsch. In a small bowl, blend together cornflour and 1 tablespoon of water. Add to the fondue pot and continue to cook, stirring, until the mixture thickens. Transfer the fondue pot to the lighted spirit burner. Serve with the chocolate cake to dip in.

Serves 4.

PRALINE FONDUE

115g (4oz/½ cup) caster sugar
115g (4oz/¾ cup) blanched almonds
225g (8oz) white chocolate
155ml (5fl oz/⅔ cup) double cream
few drops vanilla essence
cubes of cake and a selection of fresh fruit, to serve

To make praline, oil a baking sheet. Put sugar and almonds into a small heavy-based saucepan. Place over a low heat and leave until sugar becomes liquid and golden. Pour at once on to oiled baking sheet, then leave to cool and harden for 15 minutes.

Coarsely break up praline, then put into a blender or food processor and process until finely ground.

Put chocolate and cream into a fondue pot and heat gently until chocolate melts, stirring all the time. Stir in praline and flavour with a few drops of essence. Serve with cubes of cake and pieces of fresh fruit.

Serves 6.

TIRAMISU FONDUE

250g (9oz) mascarpone cheese
2 tablespoons rum
100g (3½oz) plain chocolate
1 tablespoon coffee granules
1 tablespoon caster sugar (optional)
TO SERVE:
squares of panettone
Italian sponge finger biscuits
strawberries

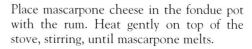

Place mascarpone cheese in the fondue pot with the rum. Heat gently on top of the stove, stirring, until mascarpone melts.

Break up chocolate into small pieces and add to the fondue pot. Continue to heat gently until chocolate melts.

Add coffee granules and stir until mixture is smooth. Taste the fondue and add sugar if desired. Transfer the fondue pot to the lighted spirit burner and serve with panettone, sponge fingers and strawberries.

Serves 4.

BANOFFEE FONDUE

250g (9oz) vanilla fudge
300ml (10fl oz/1¼ cups) double cream
sliced bananas, to serve
MINI CHOCOLATE MUFFINS:
40g (1½oz) plain chocolate
150g (5oz/1¼ cups) plain flour
1½ teaspoons baking powder
pinch salt
½ teaspoon ground cinnamon
50g (2oz/¼ cup) caster sugar
1 egg
115ml (4fl oz/½ cup) milk
50g (2oz/¼ cup) butter, melted and cooled slightly

Preheat the oven to 200C (400F/Gas 6).

Arrange 20 petit-four cases on a baking sheet. To make the muffins, chop the chocolate into small pieces. Sift the flour, baking powder, salt and cinnamon into a bowl. In another bowl, whisk together the sugar, egg, milk and melted butter. Add the dry ingredients and the chocolate and fold together quickly and lightly until just combined. Divide the mixture between the petit-four cases and bake in the oven for 15 minutes or until well risen and golden. Transfer to a wire rack to cool.

To make the fondue, place the fudge and cream in the fondue pot and heat gently, stirring until melted and smooth. Transfer the fondue pot to the lighted burner. To serve, spear the banana and muffin cakes on to bamboo skewers or fondue forks.

Serves 6.

CAPPUCCINO FONDUE

225g (8oz) white chocolate
50ml (2fl oz/¼ cup) strong espresso coffee
150ml (5fl oz/⅔ cup) double cream
drinking chocolate, for sprinkling
PISTACHIO BISCOTTI:
225g (8oz/2 cups) plain flour
1 teaspoon baking powder
pinch salt
175g (6oz/¾ cup) caster sugar
2 eggs
grated rind 1 lemon
1 tablespoon lemon juice
115g (4oz/¾ cup) blanched almonds, toasted and roughly chopped
50g (2oz/⅓ cup) shelled pistachio nuts, roughly chopped

Preheat the oven to 180C (350F/Gas 4). Line a baking sheet with non-stick parchment. To make biscotti, sift flour, baking powder and salt into a mixing bowl. Stir in sugar, eggs, lemon rind and juice and nuts. Mix together to form a firm dough. (See above.) Roll dough into a ball, cut in half and roll each portion into a roll about 3cm (1¼in) in diameter. Place rolls on the baking sheet at least 8cm (3½in) apart. Lightly flatten rolls and bake for 15-20 minutes until golden brown. Remove from oven and leave to cool and firm up for 5 minutes.

With a serrated knife, cut biscotti at an angle into 1cm (½in) thick slices. Arrange slices on baking sheet and return to the oven for a further 15 minutes, turning once. Transfer to a wire rack to cool. To make the fondue, place chocolate, coffee and cream in the fondue pot and heat gently on top of the stove until chocolate has melted and mixture is smooth. Sprinkle with drinking chocolate then transfer to the lighted spirit burner and serve with the biscotti.

Serves 4.

TOFFEE FONDUE

50g (2oz/¼ cup) butter
115g (4oz/¾ cup) demerara sugar
4 tablespoons golden syrup
400g (14oz) can evaporated milk
4 tablespoons chopped unsalted peanuts
6 teaspoons cornflour
pieces of apple, pear and banana and popcorn, to
   serve

Put butter, sugar and golden syrup into a saucepan and heat gently until mixture begins to bubble, stirring occasionally. Allow to boil for 1 minute.

Stir in evaporated milk and cook for 3-4 minutes until sauce is hot and bubbling, then add chopped nuts.

In a small bowl, blend cornflour smoothly with 2 tablespoons water. Add mixture to sauce in pan and heat until thickened, stirring. Pour into a fondue pot and place over a burner to keep warm. Serve with pieces of apple, pear and banana and popcorn.

Serves 4-6.

BUTTERSCOTCH FONDUE

50g (2oz/¼ cup) unsalted butter
175g (6oz/¾ cup) demerara sugar
2 tablespoons golden syrup
½ teaspoon grated lemon rind
1 teaspoon lemon juice
2 tablespoons cornflour
400g (14oz) can evaporated milk
fresh fruit, to serve
VANILLA COOKIES:
1 vanilla pod
115g (4oz/½ cup) unsalted butter
85g (3oz/⅓ cup) caster sugar
1 egg yolk
150g (5oz/1 cup) self-raising flour

To make the cookies, slit vanilla pod lengthways and scrape black seeds into a large bowl. (See above.) Add butter and sugar and beat together until light and fluffy. Beat in egg yolk, then stir in flour to make a stiff dough. Wrap dough in clear film and chill for 15 minutes. Preheat the oven to 190C (375F/Gas 5). Grease 2 or 3 baking sheets. Divide dough into 30 small balls and place well apart on baking sheets. Flatten slightly. Bake for 15 minutes until golden brown. Transfer to wire racks to cool.

To make fondue, place butter, sugar, syrup, lemon rind and juice in a fondue pot and heat gently until sugar has dissolved. Boil for 1 minute. Blend cornflour and 2 tablespoons of the evaporated milk. Stir remaining evaporated milk into sugar mixture. Heat until just simmering then simmer for 2-3 minutes. Stir in blended cornflour then bring to the boil, stirring, until smooth and thick. Transfer to the lighted spirit burner and serve with the cookies and fruit.

Serves 6.

FRUITS OF THE FOREST FONDUE

500g (1lb 2oz) packet of frozen fruits of the forest
  or summer fruits
4 tablespoons icing sugar
2 tablespoons crème de cassis or kirsch
2 tablespoons cornflour
200g (7oz/scant 1 cup) fromage frais
MINI LEMON CAKES:
2 eggs
115g (4oz/½ cup) softened butter
115g (4oz/½ cup) caster sugar
115g (4oz/1 cup) self-raising flour
grated rind 1 lemon
1 tablespoon lemon juice

Preheat the oven to 190C (375F/Gas 5).
Arrange 40 paper petit four cases on a baking
sheet. (See above.) To make lemon cakes,
put eggs, butter and sugar into a bowl. Sift
flour over. Add lemon rind and juice and
beat together until smooth. Put a teaspoon
of mixture in each of the petit four cases and
bake for 10-15 minutes until cooked and
firm to the touch. Leave to cool on a wire
rack before removing from the paper cases.

Process fruit and any juice in a blender or
food processor, then press through a sieve
into a fondue pot. Stir in icing sugar; heat
gently on the stove until almost simmering.
Blend together crème de cassis or kirsch and
cornflour and stir into fruit purée. Cook,
stirring, for 2-3 minutes until thickened. Stir
in fromage frais and heat gently, stirring,
until well blended. Transfer the fondue pot
to the lighted spirit burner and serve fondue
with lemon cakes for dipping.

Serves 6.

HOT BERRY COMPOTE

500g (1lb 2oz) mixed summer fruits such as
  redcurrants, blackcurrants and raspberries
115g (4oz/½ cup) caster sugar
pinch mixed spice
6 teaspoons cornflour
LANGUE DE CHAT BISCUITS:
115g (4oz/½ cup) butter
115g (4oz/½ cup) caster sugar
2 eggs
175g (6oz/1½ cups) self-raising flour

To make biscuits, preheat oven to 220C
(425F/Gas 7). Grease 2 or 3 baking sheets.
Beat butter and sugar together until pale and
fluffy; beat in eggs and work in flour.

Put mixture into a piping bag fitted with a
1cm (½in) plain nozzle and pipe 6cm (2½in)
fingers on to greased baking sheets (spaced
well apart) to make a batch of 24-30. Bake in
the oven for about 8 minutes until light
golden. Cool on a wire rack.

To make fondue, put fruits into a saucepan
with sugar and 150ml (5fl oz/⅔ cup) water
and cook gently until tender. Crush fruits
slightly with a potato masher and add mixed
spice. In a small bowl, blend cornflour
smoothly with a little water. Add to fruit in
pan and cook until thickened, stirring all the
time. Pour into a fondue pot and place over
a lighted spirit burner. Serve with langue de
chat biscuits.

Serves 6.

LEMON MERINGUE FONDUE

4 tablespoons cornflour
400ml (14fl oz/1¾ cups) coconut milk
grated rind and juice 2 lemons
50g (2oz/¼ cup) caster sugar
pieces of mango, to serve
MERINGUES:
2 egg whites
115g (4oz/½ cup) caster sugar
½ teaspoon vanilla extract

Preheat the oven to 110C (225F/Gas ¼). Line 2 or 3 baking sheets with non-stick paper. Put egg whites in a large clean bowl and whisk until meringue holds soft peaks.

Add sugar, 1 tablespoonful at a time, whisking well after each addition. Continue whisking until stiff and glossy. Fold in vanilla with a rubber spatula. Put 24 teaspoonfuls of mixture on to lined baking sheets. Bake for 1-1½ hours until dry and crisp. Turn off oven and leave meringues in oven to cool. Remove from the paper when cool.

To make the fondue, put cornflour and a little of the coconut milk in the fondue pot and stir to make a paste. Stir in remaining coconut milk. Bring to the boil on top of the stove, stirring, and continue to cook for 2-3 minutes until thickened. Remove from heat and add lemon rind and juice and sugar. Reheat then transfer the fondue pot to the lighted spirit burner. Serve with the mango and meringues.

Serves 4-6.

RASPBERRY CREAM

450g (1lb) raspberries, thawed if frozen
4 teaspoons cornflour
300ml (10fl oz/1¼ cups) single cream
50g (2oz/⅓ cup) icing sugar
3 tablespoons Framboise (optional)
QUICK MERINGUES:
2 egg whites
115g (4oz/⅔ cup) icing sugar

Rub raspberries through a sieve and discard seeds. Keep purée on one side.

To make the meringues, preheat oven to 160C (325F/Gas 3). Line a baking sheet with non-stick paper. Place egg whites and icing sugar in a bowl over a pan of hot water and with an electric whisk, whisk until mixture is stiff and standing in peaks. Place mixture in a piping bag fitted with a 1cm (½in) star nozzle and pile small blobs on to lined baking sheet. Bake in the oven for 10-15 minutes until crisp on the outside. Allow to cool before removing from paper.

In a saucepan, blend the cornflour smoothly with a little of the cream. Stir in the remainder and add sugar and raspberry purée. Cook over a gentle heat until smooth and thickened. Stir in the Framboise, if desired, then pour into a fondue pot and serve with small meringues. Serve hot or cold.

Serves 4-6.

SWEET CHERRY COMPOTE

2 x 425g (15oz) cans red cherries
6 teaspoons cornflour
85g (3oz/⅓ cup) caster sugar
3 tablespoons cherry brandy
ice cream, to serve
FANCY CAKES:
50g (2oz/¼ cup) butter
2 eggs, separated
50g (2oz/¼ cup) caster sugar
50g (2oz/½ cup) plain flour
grated rind ½ lemon

To make cakes, preheat oven to 190C (375F/Gas 5). Grease and flour 12 bun tins. Warm butter in a pan until just melting.

Whisk egg yolks and sugar until pale and creamy. Lightly fold in sifted flour, lemon rind and butter until thoroughly mixed. Whisk egg whites until stiff and fold into mixture. Spoon mixture into greased and floured bun tins. Bake in the oven for 10 minutes or until golden and firm to touch. Turn out and cool on a wire rack.

To make the compote, drain cherries, reserving juice, and remove stones. In a saucepan, blend cornflour smoothly with a little of the reserved juice, then add the remainder and stir in sugar. Cook over a medium heat until the sauce has thickened, stirring all the time. Stir in cherries and brandy. Reheat, then pour into the fondue pot over a lighted spirit burner. Serve with a small ladle to pour over ice cream and fancy cakes.

Serves 6.

FRUIT SURPRISES

350g (12oz) frozen puff pastry, thawed
225g (8oz) can pineapple slices, drained and juice reserved
50g (2oz/⅓ cup) glacé cherries, chopped
25g (1oz) angelica, chopped
oil, for cooking
RUM SAUCE:
4 oranges
3 teaspoons cornflour
50g (2oz/⅓ cup) demerara sugar
25g (1oz/6 teaspoons) butter, diced
4 tablespoons dark rum

On a lightly floured surface, roll out pastry thinly; cut into eighteen 7.5cm (3in) squares.

Chop pineapple and mix with cherries and angelica. Place a teaspoonful of mixture in the centre of each pastry square. Dampen the edges with water and fold over to form triangles; seal well and fork the edges. Refrigerate until needed. Heat the oil in the fondue pot on top of the stove then transfer to the lighted spirit burner. Cook the pastry triangles in the hot oil, lifting out with Chinese wire strainers, if possible.

To make rum sauce, finely grate rind from one of the oranges, then squeeze juice from all of them. Put cornflour in a saucepan, add reserved pineapple juice and blend together smoothly. Add sugar and orange juice and stir well. Bring to the boil, stirring all the time and simmer for 2 minutes. Whisk in butter, orange rind and rum. Serve hot with the hot pastry triangles.

Serves 6.

STRAWBERRY ROULÉ DIP

400g (14oz) can strawberries, drained
225g (8oz) strawberry roulé cheese
150ml (5fl oz/⅔ cup) double cream
fresh strawberries and Quick Almond Sponge (see
    page 81), to serve

Put strawberries and cheese into a blender or
food processor and blend until smooth.

In a bowl, whip the cream until softly
peaking, the fold in the strawberry cheese
mixture. Turn mixture into a serving bowl.

Hull strawberries, if desired, and arrange on
a serving plate with cubes of almond sponge.
Spear a strawberry or a piece of sponge on
fondue forks and dunk in the dip.

Serves 4-6.

SPICED APRICOT FONDUE

2 x 400g (14oz) cans apricot halves in natural juice
1 sachet wine mulling spices
2 tablespoons cornflour
300g (10oz/1¼ cups) fromage frais
kiwi fruit, to serve
ALMOND MACAROONS:
2 large egg whites
85g (3oz/¼ cup) ground almonds
115g (4oz/½ cup) caster sugar
1 tablespoon cornflour
few drops almond essence
24 split blanched almonds

Preheat the oven to 190C (375F/Gas 5). Line
2 or 3 baking sheets with non-stick paper.

Make the macaroons. Reserve 2 teaspoons of
egg white for brushing. In a large bowl, whisk
remaining egg whites until frothy. (See
above.) Stir in ground almonds, sugar,
cornflour and almond essence. Mix together
thoroughly. Place 24 small spoonfuls of
mixture on to lined baking sheets. Smooth
out slightly with the back of a spoon. Place a
split blanched almond in centre of each
macaroon and brush the top with reserved
egg white. Bake for 10-15 minutes until a
pale golden brown. Leave for 5 minutes then
transfer to a wire rack to cool.

Place apricots and juice in fondue pot with
spice sachet. Heat until simmering then
remove from heat and leave to cool. Remove
sachet and place apricots and juice in a
blender or food processor. Process to a purée
and return to fondue pot. Reheat gently. In a
small bowl, blend cornflour with a little water.
Add to apricot purée and continue to heat,
stirring, until thickened. Stir in fromage frais
then transfer fondue pot to lighted burner.
Serve with kiwi fruit and macaroons.

Serves 4-6.

SPICED PLUM PURÉE

700g (1½lb) red or yellow plums
85g (3oz/½ cup) sugar
½ teaspoon ground cinnamon
4 teaspoons cornflour
2 tablespoons ginger wine
Lemon Sponge (see page 86), and slices of apple and
    pear, to serve

Cut plums in half; discard stones. Put plums into a saucepan with sugar and cinnamon and 300ml (10fl oz/1¼ cups) water. Cover and simmer for 15 minutes.

Press the fruit mixture through a sieve into a fondue pot.

In a small bowl, blend cornflour smoothly with wine and stir into plum purée. Heat gently, stirring until thickened. Serve with small squares of lemon sponge and slices of apple and pear to dip into the purée.

Serves 4-6.

APRICOT YOGURT DIP

225g (8oz) ready-to-eat dried apricots
2 tablespoons Amaretto liqueur
150ml (5fl oz/⅔ cup) natural yogurt
QUICK ALMOND SPONGE:
2 eggs
115g (4oz/½ cup) soft tub margarine
115g (4oz/½ cup) caster sugar
115g (4oz/1 cup) self-raising flour
pinch baking powder
few drops almond essence

Put apricots into a bowl, cover with 300ml (10fl oz/1¼ cups) water and leave to soak for 2-3 hours.

To make quick almond sponge, preheat oven to 180C (350F/Gas 4). Grease a 17.5cm (7in) shallow, square cake tin. Put all the ingredients for sponge into a bowl and beat with a wooden spoon for 3 minutes. Turn mixture into greased tin and bake in the oven for 25 minutes or until golden brown and firm to the touch. Turn on to a wire rack and leave to cool. Cut into small squares when cold.

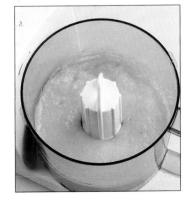

Drain apricots (reserving liquor) and put into a blender or food processor with the Amaretto and yogurt. Blend until smooth. If mixture is a little too thick, add a small amount of reserved apricot liquor. Spoon into a fondue pot and heat over a lighted spirit burner to serve warm with the pieces of cake.

Serves 4-6.

Note: The dip can also be served cold.

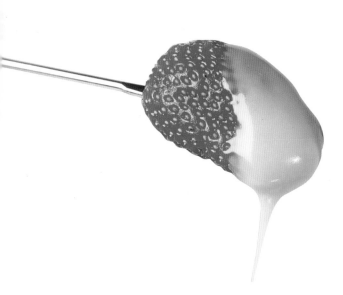

STRAWBERRY & CREAM FONDUE

50g (2oz/½ cup) strawberries
icing sugar
350g (13oz) white chocolate
225ml (8fl oz/1 cup) double cream
2 tablespoons framboise or kirsch
fresh strawberries, to serve

Place strawberries in a liquidiser or food processor and process until smooth. Press through a sieve into a bowl. Add icing sugar to taste.

Roughly chop or break up chocolate into pieces and place in the fondue pot. Add the double cream. Over a low heat, heat gently, stirring continuously, until chocolate melts. Add the framboise or kirsch, and stir until smooth.

Place the fondue pot over a lighted spirit burner to keep warm. Swirl the strawberry purée on the surface of the cream sauce. Serve with fresh strawberries.

Serves 6.

BLACKCURRANT FONDUE

700g (1½lb) blackcurrants, topped and tailed if fresh; thawed if frozen
115g (4oz/½ cup) caster sugar
3 teaspoons cornflour
2 tablespoons single cream
4 tablespoons Cassis
HAZELNUT MACAROONS:
2 egg whites
115g (4oz/½ cup) light soft brown sugar
175g (6oz/1⅔ cups) ground hazelnuts
25g (1oz/¼ cup) finely chopped hazelnuts

To make macaroons, preheat oven to 180C (350F/Gas 4). Line 3 baking sheets with non-stick paper. Whisk egg whites until softly peaking. Fold in sugar and ground nuts.

Place spoonfuls on to lined baking sheets to make a total of 24. Sprinkle with chopped nuts and bake in the oven for 15-20 minutes until crisp and firm to the touch.

To make the fondue, put blackcurrants into a saucepan with sugar and 150ml (5fl oz/⅔ cup) water and cook gently until tender. Press mixture through a sieve into a fondue pot. In a small bowl, blend cornflour smoothly with cream and stir into the purée together with Cassis. Reheat until thickened, stirring frequently. Serve with hazelnut macaroons.

Serves 4-6.

FRUIT FRITTERS

2 bananas, cut into 2.5cm (1in) pieces
2 eating apples, cored and cut into chunks
2 teaspoons lemon juice
1 small, fresh pineapple, peeled and cut into chunks
oil, for cooking
115g (4oz/½ cup) caster sugar mixed with
 1 teaspoon ground cinnamon, to serve
BATTER:
125g (4oz/1 cup) plain flour
pinch salt
1 egg
155ml (5fl oz/⅔ cup) milk

Toss bananas and apples in lemon juice, then arrange on a plate with pineapple.

To make batter, sift flour and salt into a bowl. Beat in egg, then gradually add milk, beating to make a smooth batter. Heat oil in the fondue pot on top of the stove then transfer to the lighted spirit burner.

The fritters are cooked at the table by spearing the fruit with a fondue fork, dipping it in the batter and cooking in the hot oil. Pat each fritter on paper towels, then dip in cinnamon sugar mixture before eating.

Serves 6.

Note: To add extra colour, decorate cinnamon sugar with a sprig of mint or pineapple leaves, if desired.

PEPPERMINT FONDUE

550ml (20fl oz/2½ cups) single cream
150g (5oz/1 cup) icing sugar
6 teaspoons cornflour
peppermint essence, to taste
MINI CHOCOLATE CAKES:
2 eggs
115g (4oz/½ cup) soft tub margarine
115g (4oz/½ cup) caster sugar
115g (4oz/1 cup) self-raising flour
6 teaspoons cocoa
3 teaspoons milk

To make chocolate cakes, preheat oven to 190C (375F/Gas 5). Put all ingredients into a bowl and beat together until smooth.

Put teaspoonfuls of mixture into 40 petits fours cases on a baking sheet. Bake in the oven for 15 minutes until cooked. Leave to cool on a wire rack before removing from paper cases.

Put cream and sugar into a saucepan and heat gently until almost boiling. Blend cornflour smoothly with 1 tablespoon water, add to cream and continue to heat, stirring all the time until thickened. Add essence, to taste, then pour into a fondue pot and serve hot with mini chocolate cakes.

Serves 6.

COCONUT DIP

85g (3oz/1 cup) desiccated coconut
50g (2oz) creamed coconut, chopped
50g (2oz/¼ cup) sugar
4 teaspoons cornflour
150ml (5fl oz/⅔ cup) single cream
MINI FLAPJACKS:
115g (4oz/½ cup) margarine
4 tablespoons clear honey
85g (3oz/½ cup) soft brown sugar
225g (8oz/2 cups) porridge oats
50g (2oz/⅓ cup) chopped blanched almonds

To make flapjacks, preheat oven to 180C (350F/Gas 4). In a saucepan, melt margarine, honey and sugar. Add oats and nuts; mix well.

Using a teaspoon, spoon mixture into 48 petits fours cases on a baking sheet. Bake in the oven for 20 minutes until golden. Leave to cool.

To make dip, put desiccated coconut in a saucepan with 500ml (18fl oz/2¼ cups) water, the creamed coconut and sugar. Bring to the boil and simmer for 10 minutes. Strain mixture into a bowl, pressing mixture thoroughly to extract all liquid. In a fondue pot, blend cornflour smoothly with cream, then add coconut liquid and cook over a gentle heat until thickened, stirring all the time. Serve warm with mini flapjacks.

Serves 6.

SABAYON SAUCE

4 large, ripe, firm eating pears
115ml (4fl oz/½ cup) Marsala
3 egg yolks
85g (3oz/⅓ cup) caster sugar
3 teaspoons brandy

Preheat oven to 180C (350F/Gas 4). Peel, halve and core pears and slice thickly. Put in an ovenproof dish, pour Marsala over, then cover and bake in the oven for 20 minutes.

Drain off juice from pears and reserve. Place egg yolks and sugar in a bowl and whisk until pale and frothy. Add reserved juice from pears, then place bowl over a pan of simmering water and whisk until mixture is thick.

Remove bowl from pan, stir in brandy and serve immediately, with the pear slices for dipping.

Serves 4-6.

GOOSEBERRY WINE FONDUE

700g (1½lb) gooseberries, topped and tailed
115g (4oz/1½ cup) caster sugar
150ml (5fl oz/⅔ cup) dry white wine
2 teaspoons cornflour
2 tablespoons single cream
BRANDY SNAPS:
50g (2oz/¼ cup) butter
115g (4oz/⅓ cup) demerara sugar
115g (4oz/2 tablespoons) golden syrup
115g (4oz/½ cup) plain flour
½ teaspoon ground ginger

To make brandy snaps, preheat oven to 180C (350F/Gas 4). Melt butter, sugar and golden syrup in a saucepan.

Cool slightly, then beat in flour and ginger. Place 4 teaspoonfuls of mixture on to a baking sheet, spaced well apart, and bake in the oven for 10 minutes. Repeat with remaining mixture, to make a total of 24. Leave each batch to cool slightly on baking sheet before removing with a palette knife and rolling around clean, greased pencils or chopsticks. Allow to cool and set before removing.

Put gooseberries into a saucepan with sugar and wine. Simmer until tender. Reserve a few gooseberries for decoration, then pass remainder through a sieve to make a purée. In a fondue pot, blend cornflour smoothly with cream. Stir in gooseberry purée, then heat until smooth and thick, stirring frequently. Decorate with reserved gooseberries and serve with brandy snaps.

Serves 4-6.

RHUBARB & CUSTARD FONDUE

550g (1¼lb) canned rhubarb in syrup
450g (1lb) carton ready-made fresh custard
GINGER SPONGE:
2 eggs
115g (4oz/½ cup) softened butter
115g (4oz/½ cup) golden caster sugar
115g (4oz/1 cup) self-raising flour
1 teaspoon ground ginger
pinch baking powder
2 pieces ginger from a jar of stem ginger in syrup, finely chopped
1 tablespoon syrup from the ginger jar

Preheat oven to 180C (350F/Gas 4). Grease a 17.5cm (7in) shallow, square cake tin.

To make the ginger sponge, put eggs, butter and caster sugar in a bowl. Sift flour, ginger and baking powder into the bowl. Add chopped ginger and syrup and beat together until thoroughly blended. (See above.) Turn the mixture into the prepared tin and bake for 25 minutes or until golden and firm to the touch. Leave in the tin for 5 minutes then turn out on to a wire rack to cool. Cut into small squares when cold.

To make the fondue, drain rhubarb and place in a blender or food processor. Process to a purée then place in the fondue pot with the custard. Heat on top of the stove until hot but not boiling. Transfer the fondue pot to the lighted spirit burner and serve with the ginger sponge.

Serves 4-6.

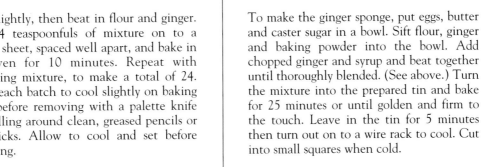

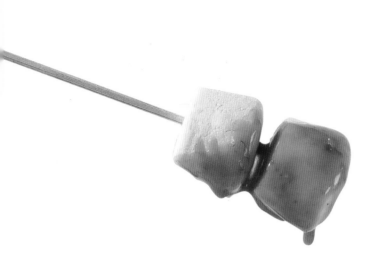

MARSHMALLOW FONDUE

225g (8oz) marshmallows
150ml (5fl oz/⅔ cup) bottled raspberry or
   strawberry coulis
150ml (5fl oz/⅔ cup) double cream
1-2 tablespoons lemon juice (optional)
TO SERVE:
marshmallows
sponge fingers
strawberries

Using wet scissors, snip marshmallows into pieces and place in the fondue pot.

Add fruit coulis and cream. Place over a very low heat and cook gently, stirring, until marshmallows have melted and mixture is smooth.

Add lemon juice, to taste, if desired. Transfer the fondue pot to the lighted spirit burner and serve with marshmallows, sponge fingers and strawberries.

Serves 4.

DRAMBUIE CREAM FONDUE

4 teaspoons cornflour
300ml (10fl oz/1¼ cups) double cream
3 teaspoons caster sugar
3 tablespoons Drambuie
3 oranges, peeled and segmented, to serve
LEMON SPONGE:
2 eggs
115g (4oz/½ cup) soft tub margarine
115g (4oz/½ cup) caster sugar
115g (4oz/1 cup) self-raising flour
pinch baking powder
finely grated rind and juice ½ lemon

Preheat oven to 180C (350F/Gas 4). Put all ingredients for sponge in a bowl.

Beat together for 3 minutes. Grease a 17.5cm (7in) shallow, square cake tin. Turn mixture into greased cake tin. Bake in the oven for 25 minutes or until golden and firm to the touch. Turn on to a wire rack and leave to cool. Cut into small squares when cold.

To make fondue, in a saucepan, blend cornflour smoothly with cream. Cook over gentle heat until thickened and smooth, stirring all the time. Stir in sugar and Drambuie, then pour into a serving dish. Serve with segments of orange and squares of lemon sponge.

Serves 6.

Note: Cut the rind from oranges into strips to decorate, if desired.

SAUCES
& SALADS

ROUILLE

2 slices white bread, crusts removed
2 red peppers, seeded and quartered
2 fresh red chillies, seeded and chopped
2 cloves garlic, crushed
olive oil

Place bread in a shallow dish with 3-4 tablespoons cold water and soak for 10 minutes.

Grill red pepper quarters, skin side up, until the skin is charred and blistered. Place in a plastic bag until cool enough to handle. Peel off skins and chop flesh roughly.

Place red pepper flesh in a blender or food processor. Drain the bread and squeeze out the excess moisture. Add to peppers with chillies and garlic. Process to a coarse paste then gradually add enough olive oil to give the desired consistency. Transfer to small serving bowls.

Serves 4-6.

CHILLI TOMATO SAUCE

1 onion
2 sticks celery
1 clove garlic
1 red pepper
1 fresh red chilli
2 tablespoons oil
400g (14oz) canned chopped tomatoes
1 teaspoon molasses or soft brown sugar
salt and freshly ground black pepper
chopped fresh coriander, to garnish

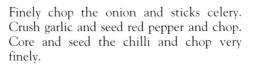

Finely chop the onion and sticks celery. Crush garlic and seed red pepper and chop. Core and seed the chilli and chop very finely.

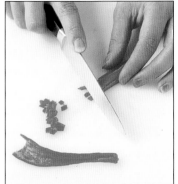

Heat oil in a saucepan. Add onion, celery, garlic and red pepper and cook for 10 minutes until soft. Add chilli, tomatoes and molasses and season with salt and pepper.

Bring to the boil, cover and simmer gently for 20-30 minutes until thickened and well blended. Garnish with chopped coriander.

Serves 4-6.

TWO MAYONNAISES

CUMBERLAND SAUCE

SAFFRON MAYONNAISE:
150ml (5fl oz/⅔ cup) fish stock
½ teaspoon saffron strands
150ml (5fl oz/⅔ cup) mayonnaise
1 teaspoon lemon juice
salt and freshly ground black pepper

AIOLI:
50ml (5fl oz/⅔ cup) mayonnaise
2 cloves garlic, crushed
1 teaspoon Dijon mustard
salt and freshly ground black pepper (optional)

To make the saffron mayonnaise, put fish stock in a saucepan and bring to the boil.

Boil until reduced to 1 tablespoon. Add saffron strands and leave to cool. Strain stock into a bowl and stir in mayonnaise. Add lemon juice and season with salt and pepper. (Salt will not be needed if the fish stock was salty.) Spoon into a serving bowl, cover and chill until required.

To make the aioli, place mayonnaise, garlic and mustard in a bowl. Mix together and season with salt and pepper, if desired. Transfer to a serving bowl, cover and chill until required. Set aside.

Serves 4.

1 shallot
1 orange
1 lemon
115g (4oz/⅓ cup) redcurrant jelly
1 teaspoon Dijon mustard
70ml (2½fl oz/⅓ cup) port
1 teaspoon arrowroot

Chop shallot very finely and place in a saucepan. With a peeler, remove the rind of orange and lemon.

Cut into very fine strips and add to the pan. Cover with cold water, bring to the boil and cook for 5 minutes. Drain and set aside. Meanwhile, halve orange and lemon and squeeze juice. Set aside. Add redcurrant jelly to the pan and heat gently, stirring until melted.

Stir in mustard, port, juice of orange and lemon and blanched rind and shallot. Cook for about 5 minutes. In a small bowl, mix arrowroot to a paste with a 1 tablespoon of cold water. Add to the sauce in the pan. Simmer for a further 2-3 minutes until slightly thickened then leave to cool before serving.

Serves 4.

TOMATO & OLIVE SALSA

4 plum tomatoes
175g (6oz/1¼ cups) mixed pitted green and black
  olives, roughly chopped
1 small red onion, finely chopped
1 fresh red chilli, seeded and finely chopped
2 tablespoons olive oil
salt and freshly ground black pepper

To peel the tomatoes, cut a cross in the rounded side of each tomato.

Place them in a bowl and pour boiling water over to cover. Leave for 1 minute then drain and cover with cold water. Leave for 1 more minute, then remove and peel. Cut tomatoes into quarters and remove cores, then cut tomato flesh into tiny dice and place in a bowl.

Add olives, onion and chilli to tomatoes in the bowl. Stir in olive oil and season with salt and pepper. Transfer to a serving bowl and serve.

Serves 4.

AVOCADO & MELON SALSA

1 ripe avocado
½ canteloupe melon
juice 1 lime
4 spring onions, very finely chopped
1 fresh red chilli, seeded and very finely chopped
salt and freshly ground black pepper
mint leaves, to garnish

Cut the avocado in half. Remove the stone and peel off the skin.

Remove seeds from melon and cut away skin. Cut avocado and melon into small dice and place in a bowl with lime juice. Toss together well. Add spring onions and chilli. Season with salt and pepper.

Cover closely with clear film and leave to stand for 30 minutes. (Do not leave for longer than this or the avocado will discolour.) Transfer to a serving dish. Roughly tear or chop the mint leaves and scatter over the salsa before serving.

Serves 4.

VARIATION: Any type of melon can be used as long as it is ripe and has a good flavour. You should have 225g (8oz) melon after peeling and seeding.

CHOW MEIN SALAD

COUSCOUS SALAD

115g (4oz) Chinese medium egg noodles
115g (4oz) mange-tout
175g (6oz) fresh beansprouts
½ bunch spring onions, chopped
1 red pepper, seeded and sliced
115g (4oz) button mushrooms, sliced
1 small Little Gem lettuce, shredded
SESAME DRESSING:
4 tablespoons sunflower oil
2 tablespoons lemon juice
3 teaspoons soy sauce
2.5cm (1in) piece of fresh root ginger
2 tablespoons sesame seeds

Break up noodles and cook in boiling, salted water for 5-6 minutes.

Drain noodles and leave to cool. Top and tail mange-tout, then break in half and put into a bowl. Pour over enough boiling water to cover and leave to stand for 2 minutes; drain and cool. Put noodles and mange-tout into a salad bowl and add remaining salad ingredients.

In a bowl, combine oil, lemon juice and soy sauce. Peel and cut ginger into very thin slivers and add to bowl. Mix ingredients together thoroughly and pour over salad. Toss together. Sprinkle with sesame seeds just before serving.

Serves 6-8.

3 tablespoons olive oil
5 spring onions, chopped
1 clove garlic, crushed
1 teaspoon ground cumin
350ml (12fl oz/1½ cups) vegetable stock
175g (6oz/1 cup) couscous
2 tomatoes, peeled and chopped
4 tablespoons chopped fresh parsley
4 tablespoons chopped fresh mint
1 fresh green chilli, seeded and finely chopped
2 tablespoons lemon juice
salt and freshly ground black pepper
toasted pine nuts and grated lemon rind, to garnish

Heat oil in a saucepan. Add spring onions and garlic.

Stir in cumin. Add stock and bring to the boil. Remove the pan from the heat and stir in couscous. Leave to stand for 10 minutes until couscous has absorbed all the liquid. Fluff up with a fork and transfer to a serving dish.

Leave to cool then stir in tomatoes, parsley, mint, chilli and lemon juice. Season with salt and pepper. Leave to stand for up to 1 hour to allow the flavours to develop. Scatter pine nuts and lemon rind over and serve.

Serves 4.

ORANGE & RED ONION SALAD

6 oranges
2 small red onions
1 tablespoon cumin seeds
1 teaspoon coarsely ground black pepper
1 tablespoon chopped fresh mint
6 tablespoons olive oil
salt
mint sprigs and black olives, to garnish

Working over a bowl to catch the juice, cut the skin away from oranges, removing the pith.

With a sharp knife, slice the oranges thinly. Slice onions across thinly, into rings, then separate the layers of the rings. Arrange the orange and onion slices in layers in a shallow dish. Sprinkle each layer with cumin seeds, black pepper, mint, olive oil and salt to taste.

Pour any orange juice saved from slicing oranges over the salad. Leave in a cool place for about 2 hours, for the flavours to develop. Just before serving, scatter the salad with mint sprigs and black olives.

Serves 6.

VARIATION: Slices of fennel may be added to this salad.

SUMMER VEGETABLE SALAD

350g (12oz) aubergine, diced
salt and freshly ground black pepper
3 tablespoons olive oil
1 Spanish onion, sliced
350g (12oz) courgettes, sliced
1 red pepper, seeded and cut into chunks
1 green pepper, seeded and cut into chunks
1 yellow pepper, seeded and cut into chunks
3 tomatoes, peeled and chopped
1 tablespoon chopped fresh basil
1 tablespoon chopped fresh parsley (optional)

Put aubergine into a colander, sprinkle with salt and leave to stand for 30 minutes. Rinse, drain and pat dry.

Heat oil in a large frying pan, add aubergine and onion and cook over medium heat for 5 minutes. Add courgettes and peppers; cook over a low heat for 15 minutes, turning occasionally until tender.

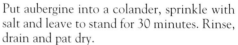

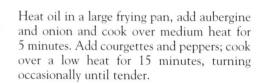

Transfer vegetables to a bowl, stir in tomatoes, basil and seasoning. Leave to cool, then chill. Serve sprinkled with chopped parsley, if desired.

Serves 6.

CARIBBEAN COLESLAW

1 red-leafed lettuce, such as oakleaf
½ iceberg lettuce, shredded
5 sticks celery, finely sliced
175g (6oz) carrots, grated
½ small pineapple, cut into chunks
85g (3oz) fresh dates, stoned and chopped
50g (2oz) walnuts or pecans, chopped
LIME DRESSING:
3 tablespoons mayonnaise
finely grated rind and juice 1 lime
6 teaspoons sunflower oil
salt and freshly ground black pepper

Line a large salad bowl or platter with red-leafed lettuce.

In a bowl, put the remaining salad ingredients, except the nuts, and mix together. Mix dressing ingredients together, then pour over salad and toss lightly.

Spoon salad into the prepared bowl or on to the platter and sprinkle with walnuts or pecans before serving.

Serves 6.

ORIENTAL GREEN SALAD

115g (4oz) mange-tout, trimmed and halved
1 small head Chinese leaves
8 spring onions, roughly chopped
1 green pepper, seeded and sliced
½ small cucumber
115g (4oz/2 cups) beansprouts
2 tablespoons chopped roasted cashew nuts, and
  2 tablespoons chopped fresh coriander, to garnish
GINGER & CHILLI DRESSING:
2.5cm (1in) piece fresh root ginger, grated
1 clove garlic, crushed
1 fresh red chilli, seeded and finely chopped
1 teaspoon clear honey
grated rind and juice 1 lime
2 tablespoons oil
1 tablespoon soy sauce

Bring a pan of water to the boil, add mange-tout, cook for 2 minutes then drain and refresh in cold water. (See above.) Drain again and place in a bowl. Finely shred Chinese leaves and add to the bowl with the spring onions and green pepper.

Peel cucumber, cut in half lengthways and slice thinly. Add to the bowl with beansprouts. To make the dressing, whisk together ginger, garlic, chilli, honey, lime rind and juice, oil and soy sauce. Pour over the salad and mix well. Transfer to a serving bowl. Before serving, scatter over chopped cashew nuts and coriander.

Serves 4-6.

BEAN SALAD

400g (14oz) canned black-eyed beans
400g (14oz) canned red kidney beans
4 sticks celery, chopped
1 green pepper, seeded and roughly chopped
1 small red onion, finely chopped
4 tablespoons olive oil
1 tablespoon lime juice
1 teaspoon sugar
½-1 teaspoon hot pepper sauce
salt and freshly ground black pepper
2 tablespoons chopped fresh parsley

Drain and rinse black-eyed beans and red kidney beans. Place in a bowl.

Add the celery, green pepper and onion to the beans.

In a bowl, mix together olive oil, lime juice, sugar and hot pepper sauce. Season with salt and pepper. Pour over the bean mixture and mix well. Set aside for 30 minutes then transfer to a serving dish. Scatter with chopped parsley and serve.

Serves 4-6.

VARIATIONS: The combination of beans can be varied according to preference and what is available.

RICE & SPINACH SALAD

350g (12oz/2½ cups) long-grain rice
2 tablespoons oil
1 bunch spring onions, chopped
225g (8oz) frozen chopped spinach, thawed and well drained
salt and freshly ground black pepper
slice of lemon, to garnish

In a medium saucepan, bring 900ml (32fl oz/4 cups) salted water to the boil. Keep water simmering while adding rice, then cover and cook for 15 minutes until rice is soft and water absorbed.

In a large saucepan, heat oil, add onions and cook for 3-4 minutes, then stir into rice.

Add spinach and season with salt and pepper, then heat through for 1-2 minutes. Stir ingredients together and serve warm, garnished with a slice of lemon. Alternatively, serve the rice cold and fluff up with a fork before serving.

Serves 6.

INDEX